EVERYTHING LOST
IS FOUND AGAIN

EVERYTHING LOST IS FOUND AGAIN

FOUR SEASONS IN LESOTHO

WILL McGRATH

DZANC
BOOKS

DZANC BOOKS

5220 Dexter Ann Arbor Rd.
Ann Arbor, MI 48103
www.dzancbooks.org

Library of Congress Cataloging-in-Publication Data

Names: McGrath, Will, 1980- author.
Title: Everything lost is found again : four seasons in Lesotho / By Will
    McGrath.
Description: Ann Arbor, MI : Dzanc Books, 2018. | Includes bibliographical
    references.
Identifiers: LCCN 2018005799 | ISBN 9781945814624
Subjects: LCSH: McGrath, Will, 1980---Travel--Lesotho. | Lesotho--Description
    and travel. | Lesotho--Social life and customs.
Classification: LCC DT2572 .M34 2018 | DDC 868.85032--dc23
LC record available at https://lccn.loc.gov/2018005799

First Edition: November 2018
Cover design by Matthew Revert
Interior design by Leslie Vedder

Portions of this work originally appeared, sometimes in different form, in the following publications: "Jink"—*Christian Science Monitor;* "Midnight Basotho Dance Party"—*Roads & Kingdoms;* "Killing a Pig"—*Gastronomica;* "Good & Bad Joala"—*Asymptote* (Pushcart Prize nominee); "Forty-One Months"—*Bellevue Literary Review* (winner of the 2014 Felice Buckvar Prize for Nonfiction); "Ghosts in Snow & Rock"—*Sundog Lit*

Some names have been changed, to protect the innocent and the guilty.

Printed in the United States of America

10   9   8   7   6   5   4   3   2   1

CONTENTS

꧁❀꧂❀꧁❀꧂❀꧁❀꧂❀꧁❀꧂❀꧁

III. AUTUMN – GROWING UP

IV. WINTER – TAKING LEAVE

APPENDIX

For Ellen, who took me there,
and Nthabeleng, who brought me back.

*Strange things happen to them, some bitterly cruel
and some so beautiful that the faith is refired forever.*

—John Steinbeck, *The Grapes of Wrath*

*Violet learned then what she had forgotten until this moment:
that laughter is serious. More complicated, more serious than tears.*

—Toni Morrison, *Jazz*

I.
SPRING
KENA KA KHOTSO

At the border crossing, I saw a sign and copied the words into my notebook.

We hired a driver and he brought us through the lowlands, past fields of junked cars, past a sandstone quarry where men hammered rocks, formed them into pale smooth bricks, and stacked them in Jenga columns along the road: waist-high towers of shocked white stone against green grass. We climbed into vernal mountains and at a tight pass, where the land fell away into valley, a cloud had settled across the road ahead of us. It lay densely over the ground, flocculent and dirty white, rippling tufts obscuring the path.

It was sheep—several hundred, whipped onward by shepherds wrapped in heavy blankets. Our driver approached the flock slowly and then we entered, passed through a living membrane that sealed around us, sheep on all sides, bleating with exasperation as they strained to keep clear of the wheel wells. We inched forward, suspended somewhere, and then emerged into a new place. The sea closed behind us.

As we passed into Mokhotlong District, I saw another sign, same as the one at the border crossing. I checked against the words in my notebook: Kena ka khotso.

I asked the driver what it meant.

"Kena ka khotso?" he said. "That is the motto for this place. It means: Enter with peace. If you want to know about this place, then come peacefully and with eyes open. That is all you need here."

LOOKING FOR RAPITSOE

Reid and I are lost in Maseru.

Maseru, capital of Lesotho. You know the place.

He is in the white pickup truck loaded with two bright green fifty-five-gallon petrol drums. I am behind him in a low-riding minivan borrowed from a friend. There is a children's sing-along cassette stuck in the tape deck—the eject button has jammed and the volume on/off knob has been downsized from essential components—and so I'm juking through traffic to a soundtrack of high-decibel morality plays about the importance of share-share-sharing your toys. I'm following those bright green petrol drums, clinging to them, but people keep cutting me off and veering madly through intersections and attempting to sell me new windshield wipers when they can see that I have perfectly good windshield wipers. It is not raining in Maseru and perhaps it never has: it's a lambent spring day in southern Africa, in which my only thought is of destroying this sing-along cassette and flinging it into the dusty thoroughfare.

Three things happen in quick succession: my borrowed cell phone beeps once as the battery dies. It occurs to me that this may prove logistically challenging. Then the low-riding minivan abruptly halts. The anti-carjacking device—for reasons unknown, since I am not currently carjacking—has engaged with shocking righteousness. A chorus of horns strikes up behind me as I grope around the interior of the car, searching for the secret button to restart the minivan. But I cannot find the secret button because it is secret.

Reid slips through a stoplight, around a traffic circle, and is gone.

Fifteen seconds have elapsed. I lay my head against the locked steering wheel to ponder my reversal. An instant ago, I was driving a minivan and listening to children's music like any good American. Now, suddenly, I am alone and stranded in the capital city of a small African nation, without communication, without transportation, without destination.

Traffic piles up. People attempt to circumvent my marooned vehicle, driving up on the sidewalk and onto the median. Dogs weave between log-jammed cars. At my window, men laud the latest developments in leopard print steering-wheel-cover technology, all while the children's tape plangently counsels me on the importance of dental hygiene.

꒰ᵕ꒱

To rewind, briefly:

This story really begins in my bed. It was in that cool pre-dawn before consciousness fully arrives, when the room is suffused with blue light and the edges of dreams are at their haziest. In my memory, sunlight is seeping into the room and the curtains are blowing gauzily inward, but I know this cannot be entirely true since we have Venetian blinds. The brain enjoys furnishing our memories with props from forgotten Hollywood back lots.

"Hey." My wife, Ellen, is shaking me gently awake.

I crack an eyelid.

"Hey, do you want to move to Lesotho?"

I let the question settle over me. "Sure, I guess."

I close my eyes again and sink my face farther into the pillow.

Then after a moment: "What's Lesotho?"

꒰ᵕ꒱

I would learn an answer to that question, but it would be an incomplete answer at best. Later I would come to know Lesotho—it's LEH-*SOO*-TOO, if you're wondering—as the mountainous dreamland surrounded entirely by South Africa, the land of *Khotso Pula Nala,* of Moshoeshoe, of dinosaurs and double galaxies—a place where board games are carved into boulders and the phone company texts you about the king's birthday party. But I'm getting ahead of myself.

It was my wife who first brought us to Lesotho. Ellen is a cultural anthropologist who studies AIDS and orphan care, and Lesotho sits at the disquieting intersection of her research areas. The kingdom has the second highest HIV prevalence rate on the planet, 25 percent of the adult population—a figure that leads inexorably to the number of orphans in Lesotho. Of the 766,000 children in the country, around 211,000 have lost one or both parents, nearly 28 percent. Yet statistics like these often obscure more than they enlighten, painting with a macro brush at the expense of the granularity of human experience. What can a number, hovering in the abstract, really say about the character of a place?

I had recently completed a teacher training program and was eager to explore Lesotho for myself, hungry to know more of the world before embarking on a lifelong journey of high school teaching. (I use the word "embark" here because secondary education is in many ways similar to a lengthy voyage at sea. The surrounding fauna are beautiful and alien—glass-eyed and sharp-toothed, suddenly aggressive, asleep, quicksilver brilliant—and the surface beneath is in perpetual tilt. The whole enterprise is claustrophobic and thrilling and not infrequently marked by vomiting.) But my preliminary Googling of Lesotho had turned up somewhat circumscribed results: statistics that pointed toward generalized tragedy and news factoids that forever contained the descriptors "impoverished" and "landlocked." This is how the search engines of the outside world viewed it—*Lesotho is an impoverished and landlocked nation within South Africa*—and in an age mediated by internet connectivity, this becomes its own kind of truth, raising a related question along the way: if the outside world continually classifies you as tragic, poor, and penned in, do you eventually begin to see yourself that way? *At what point does perception become reality?* I would ask my students as they dozed sweetly at their desks or furtively sexted one another.

Whenever my wife and I told someone where we were headed, the first question posed was: "Is it dangerous?" People assumed sand, safaris, and jungles; assumed lions, rhinos, and giraffes; assumed malaria, assumed AIDS. (Only one of those exists in Lesotho.) "What about warlords?" people said. It became clear that the only things we had managed to import from the African continent were clichés.

Lesotho is one of the smallest fragments of an expanse of earth that stretches five thousand miles north to south, home to fifty-four countries and thousands of languages and ethnic groups. Lesotho and Libya are both technically "African" and are as similar as the United States and the United Arab Emirates. How significant is it, really, to label something in this way—to note that two places exist on a contiguous landmass, which also holds true for the Yukon and Uruguay, Siberia and Cambodia?

I can say one thing with certainty: I did not come to Lesotho to find myself. There is nothing more tedious than white people venturing into foreign territory in search of self-knowledge, in search of authenticity—which must be among the language's emptiest words. There is something deeply unsettling about people who collect the essential stuff of someone else's existence for exotic furniture in their own small-scale dramas. I did not come to Lesotho for set dressing; I came to learn about the different ways that people live.

So we moved to Lesotho, Ellen and I, to the remote eastern district of Mokhotlong, up where the scorched-red earth of the foothills gives way to wind-blasted basalt, out past the diamond mine where mechanized brontosaurs churn through the night, their cones of light illuminating lunar terrain. We would live for a year in a circular rondavel with a thatched roof (this time; I didn't know then how many times we would return to Lesotho). Ellen would travel to distant villages to see how families were adapting to the AIDS crisis while I taught at the local high school. We would both spend time working at an NGO for a woman named Nthabeleng, who came recommended, in rather understated fashion, as someone worth knowing.

We did not know much else.

We did not know Sesotho, the native language, but we did know English, the language spoken in government and education. We did not know how we would acclimate to the culture, but we knew the place was peaceful. We did not know if we would be lonely. We did not know how long we would stay. We did not know Reid and Bridget, the other Americans in town, but we would always know them after. We did not know Neo or Tseli, Baholo or Poho, Mokete or Mokati. We did not know how broken the animals were. We did not know how many coffins there would be. We did not know they would ask to pray over Ellen. We did not know I would chop wood for a funeral in my school clothes. We did not know how bright the moon, how bright the stars, how dark the night.

We did not know how joyful it all would be.

We could not have guessed.

⁂

Anyway: let me just finish my story.

Reid and I had driven down from the highlands—from Mokhotlong, on the mountainous eastern border of the country, to Maseru, on the slightly-less-mountainous western border—to accomplish two things: fill two bright green fifty-five-gallon drums with gasoline and get the white pickup fixed. Nthabeleng, our boss in Mokhotlong, had asked us to leave the white pickup for repairs with a man named Rapitsoe, a maneuver that necessitated the borrowed minivan for our return trip.

The problem: we cannot find Rapitsoe. This is because the map Nthabeleng has drawn is just lines on a scrap of napkin. And while Nthabeleng is a great hero in many ways, she is no cartographer. The streets on her napkin map have no names, which is semi-reasonable in rural Mokhotlong—where roads are called things like "that one down by the butchery"—but in Maseru, in the capital city, the names of streets are of at least moderate importance. Only later will we discover that Nthabeleng has omitted three important turns from her napkin map. Nor has she included a phone number for Rapitsoe's shop, something now irrelevant since I have no functioning phone. All finger-pointing aside, I am lost. Reid disappeared around that traffic circle fifteen minutes ago and has not resurfaced.

So here I sit, like an old Bob Dylan bootleg, stuck inside Maseru on a Friday afternoon. The enraged honking has mostly subsided; people have taken in stride that this route now includes a sidewalk detour. I briefly entertain the notion of exiting the minivan, but the traffic around me is comically dangerous. Minibuses scoot across the median while people in the street sell cheese curls in Ziploc bags and just barely avoid death-by-taxi. I take a deep breath and come to terms with my situation. There is a sense of peace, a certain freedom in being optionless, with this genial madness orbiting me. The day is warm, and there is sunlight on my face.

And then the minivan comes to life. This is because I have found the secret button to disengage the anti-carjacking device (it is a piece of floor that looks like all the other pieces of floor). Things are suddenly looking up—I am lost, yes, but I am mobile again.

I drive aimlessly through Maseru, searching for Reid and taking in the wild glory of the day. Schoolchildren in plaid uniforms run through shallow gullies just off the main road, loose-limbed and freewheeling in a way that can only be achieved on a Friday afternoon, when the weekend in all its sunny potential unfurls before them. I cruise past the Palace of Justice, then the border crossing—*Kena ka khotso*, reads the sign—and soon I have reached the spiny chaos of the taxi rank. Maseru's taxi rank is parking lot-cum-labyrinth: a tangle of impromptu shacks, wandering vendors, and hundreds of idling vehicles ready to set out for Qacha's Nek, Mohale's Hoek, Mafeteng, and Teyateyaneng. This is the jittery cerebrum of the city, minibuses and four-plus-ones darting along axons and across synapses, heading for the highlands or into South Africa. Taxi drivers laugh at their own jokes, some of them openly drinking from quarts of beer, while travelers grab last packets of food for the ride. In jury-rigged metal shacks, cockeyed and listing like ships at sea, men are cooking sausages on handmade grills. Beside them women fry fat cakes or slices of nuclear pink bologna in pools of oil. A grandmother roasts yellow-black maize cobs while sliding indeterminate chunks of street meat onto skewers.

Directly off the taxi rank runs a dense warren of merchants' stalls, a street market that coils around itself like an Escher print. There are tiny districts of barber shanties where the hair clippers are powered by car batteries, then a row of cobblers stitching shoes, then a conclave of traditional healers—*ngaka ea Sesotho*—who display shoeboxes filled with nests of dark roots, hunks of wet clay, and tiny glass bottles of colored tincture, marshaled like soldiers into rank and file. It is in this narrow and unmapped corner of the city that I will wander later—many months later—and find a snooker table in a sudden clearing, out in the open air, the green baize running flat like farmland. The snooker table is untouched by the elements, perfect and pristine, and men are hustling, inviting me into the game. The sight hits me like the half-remembered shard of a dream, but it is real—I can feel the fabric under my hand, I can hear the gentle click of the balls.

It is later, in this layered and overgrown bazaar, that I will appreciate the importance of speaking a little Sesotho, when I greet some locals clustered around an overturned cardboard box, raucously playing seven-card something. At my single phrase of Sesotho they begin trying to explain the rules of the game to me, but it is far too complex, and I would much rather just watch these four sharps go at it, slapping their cards down with fast-twitch vigor as onlookers laugh and elbow me. *Djahseethat? Helele!*

Even later still—not far from here—I will briefly become a celebrity to a yardful of shrieking teenage schoolgirls as I step out of a sports car with rising gull-wing doors, a vehicle driven by a friendly Indian man named Mohammad whom I have just met. But, as I said, that is perhaps a story for another time. Because the only thing I know right now—in this present moment, as I drift through the streets of Maseru in my low-riding minivan—is that I have found Reid.

It is an hour into our separation. By now I have made peace with, have come even to love the well-lodged children's tape that is permanently bonded to the tape player.

I can sing all the words now. And I do.

I am singing when I see those fifty-five-gallon petrol drums standing up like two neon green cooling towers. Reid has pulled the white pickup truck over in a parking lot and is squinting out toward the road, his hand shading his eyes. I pull in and hug him, surging with brotherly love, with *adelphia*. We have been searching for each other, cruising aimlessly, then waiting to be found. And now we are found, although still lost.

"You realize that Nthabeleng's map is wrong?" Reid asks me. He is holding the crumpled napkin in his hand. "I followed it all the way. It goes nowhere."

I nod. We consider our situation. Together, we can probably find our way back to the friend's house where we borrowed the minivan and cell phone, but this would leave our business unfinished. Nthabeleng has tasked us with just two things: get Rapitsoe to fix the white pickup, then fill the fifty-five-gallon drums with petrol. Driving back across the entire country to Mokhotlong with business unfinished will be unacceptable. Nthabeleng will not care that she herself provided us with a hand-drawn map going nowhere.

"So how are we going to find Rapitsoe?" Reid asks.

I shrug.

The man standing next to us in the parking lot says, "I am Rapitsoe."

Reid and I look at him. The man has been sitting here on an overturned oilcan, talking with another Mosotho, in this unnamed lot near the center of town.

"Pardon?"

"I am Rapitsoe," the man says again. His tone is matter-of-fact, almost apologetic.

The other guy nods. "This one is Rapitsoe."

Reid and I look at each other, but we both understand it to be true.

Before I go on, I need to emphasize one last thing—one of the fundamental truths of Lesotho. It is a country of two million souls, a sovereign kingdom of the African continent, but it is a small town, maybe the smallest town in the world. There is some dizzying beauty in this paradox: the towering span of the mountains, the infinite spread of the sky, the land outsized in every way, yet somehow so small—a country that is a village, a nation that is a neighborhood, a place where all paths must cross and re-cross.

"I think," says the man who is Rapitsoe, "that you are the ones for 'M'e Nthabeleng? To fix the car?"

So it was right, of course, that Nthabeleng's map was wrong. Nthabeleng is never wrong. The map did not take us to Rapitsoe's shop because Rapitsoe wasn't at his shop. He was chatting with a friend in town, despite the fact that he had an appointment. The right map would have left us with business unfinished. The map leading us nowhere was, in the end, the only proper solution.

"Yes," says Reid, "we are the ones for 'M'e Nthabeleng."

"Okay, I will take you there," he says, and without further discussion Rapitsoe jumps into the passenger seat of the minivan. He guides me out toward the edge of Maseru, with Reid and the white pickup truck behind us. We slip past single-story neighborhoods, the houses built from cinderblock, the corrugated metal roofs held in place by rocks or old tires. Soon we reach a mechanic's shop, the surrounding dirt yard filled with vehicles in various states of repair and disrepair. Rapitsoe's office is a stranded campervan up on blocks, an aluminum-sided oven, and inside he hands us two cans of Coke pulled from a Styrofoam cooler with no ice in it.

Reid and I sip our hot Cokes while the wind eddies around us, staring off in the direction of Mokhotlong. Out beyond the limit of vision, dense walls of agave sprout in the foothills, the plants looking like something from a Seussian fever dream: porcupines of flat waxy leaves, tall as a man, with thin trunks jutting from their centers and pods of extraterrestrial broccoli branching skyward. The hills plane out and then cleave into dongas, deep narrow rifts where water has cracked open the earth. Mesas stand on the horizon, mountains beyond them, and the terrain is punctuated with odd spears of rock and mammoform hills where the ancient gods plucked up the fabric of the land with cosmic fingertips. The highlands wait there like a dream.

THE UNLIKELY GRADUATION OF TSELI MOELETSI

The sound carries across the hills, a dull thumping, like someone rhythmically knocking dust from a carpet. Ellen and I are walking with Nthabeleng, heading out toward the *pitso* ground for her daughter's kindergarten graduation, strolling along the main road through Mokhotlong camptown, this rural hub of seven thousand people. The main drag is lined with merchants' shanties and caravans missing wheels, improvised offices where people notarize passports or charge mobile phones or weave hair extensions. Beyond the road, the grass hugs tightly against the earth, manicured by perpetually grazing animals. Small boulders are strewn across the rolling terrain like bocce balls. Still the sound percusses the air, a steady thwack, tedious and dispassionate.

Finally I can see the source: a young shepherd is coming up the road toward us, all ten years of him, with his donkey a few steps ahead, plodding under a load of maize meal sacks. The boy is beating his donkey with a *molamo*, a wooden shepherd's club, cranking up his tiny body and unleashing, over and over again, and with each blow a little cloud of animal hair and dandruff rises off the animal's ribs.

I can feel Nthabeleng coiling beside me. Then, as we pass them, she strikes, launching into a high-velocity stream of Sesotho invective, which sounds not unlike the ignition of a fireworks warehouse. The boy's eyes go coin-shaped. Nthabeleng is yelling some question at him, punctuated occasionally by the word *uena—you!*—and the boy is trying to put distance between them, quickening his step down the road. The donkey shuffles forward, unchanged. Nthabeleng is still yelling at him over her shoulder, and as long as we are within eyesight, and then earshot the boy lays off the carpet-beating.

"Maybe in my next life I can run a safe home for donkeys," Nthabeleng says.

Nthabeleng Lephoto is about four feet tall, a tiny dynamo, and one time she tried to strangle me. Here in the mountains, she runs a safe home for children orphaned by AIDS and directs an outreach team that ventures into the loneliest corners of this alpine district—all in service of a small local organization that fights against the ravages of HIV, which affects 25 percent of Lesotho's adults. (Compare, perhaps, against the US at 0.6 percent, or the UK at 0.2 percent.)

What can you say about Nthabeleng? She is the show-runner, the point guard, the boss of the Basotho and the *mookameli* of Mokhotlong. Above all else, she is a fixer. Can't get antiretroviral meds? She's the person to talk to. Don't have food for the baby? She'll hook you up. Need a ride to the clinic? Hop in. She sees all, hears all, knows all. Out of a sense of benevolence, she may let you think you are getting away with something. You are not. She lives in your thoughts and dreams. She knows your malfeasance before you *fease* it *mal*. She speaks better English than you do. She tells funnier jokes in her third language than you do in your first. She is ferocious in the way that only the very tiny can be. When Nthabeleng walks by construction sites, nails plunge themselves through wood. Cement mixes itself. The only way to capture even a glimpse of her true self is through the words of our great philosopher-king, the former NBA star Shaquille O'Neal—listen when he tells you: Nthabeleng Lephoto is the motherfucking Truth.

But this story isn't about Nthabeleng. It's about her daughter, Tseli, who is graduating from kindergarten today. As we amble down the main road, the sun high overhead, Nthabeleng preps us for the ceremony we are about to witness. We head out toward the grain warehouse and pass the chassis of an ancient flatbed delivery truck that has sunk into the earth, wheels and engine long gone, just the shell remaining. It is half-submerged in the landscape, sculptural now. The earth accepts all things, eventually.

We aim for the soccer pitch, the *pitso* ground. The *pitso* ground is the official gathering place in Mokhotlong, where people assemble to attend to community business—and in most rural outposts like this, the *pitso* ground doubles as the local soccer field, maybe the only flat stretch of land for miles. Two rusted rectangles stand netless at opposing ends of the grounds, attempting to frame the mountains and failing dramatically.

As we arrive, Nthabeleng comments with some measure of disgust that events like these often stretch on for hours. One local potentate after another will ramble on about what he has done for Mokhotlong, she says, while conveniently forgetting that this is a ceremony for five-year-olds. There are no seats for the children or their families and Nthabeleng wonders aloud at how the speakers have provided a large shade tent and seats for themselves but nothing for the elderly *bo-nkhono* and *bo-ntate moholo* who have shuffled out to this baking plateau to see their grandchildren graduate.

So we stand with Nthabeleng—shifting our weight, trying to create shade where there is none—and listen to self-aggrandizing Sesotho monologues. The men and women from district councils, chieftaincies, and local law enforcement agencies spout shopworn speeches about how the children are our future. As we watch the ceremony, I am trying to figure out why exactly Nthabeleng wanted us to come with her. She is openly scornful as we stand here sweltering, making snide comments about the speakers, making no effort to lower the volume of her voice, daring someone to silence her. I try to remember if people in the United States make a big deal about kindergarten graduation. I ponder the question of what, exactly, is so difficult about graduating from kindergarten. You show up. You play with glue. You nap. You go home.

The speakers now begin to call the names of the graduates, who are decked out in adorable miniature caps and gowns. The kids walk shyly up to the tent, receive their diplomas, and pose for a picture. They are uniformly terrified. Then we hear Tseli's name called. Like the children before her, she approaches the stage haltingly, trying not to trip over her gown. She looks back at us with some measure of trepidation.

Nthabeleng has darted from our side. She runs up in front of the crowd, a step behind her daughter, and begins to dance and ululate—to *lilietsa*—interrupting what has been a remarkably solemn and grandiose ceremony. Tseli seems unsure what to make of her gyrating mother. Nthabeleng starts shaking her skirt rhythmically, making the backside leap up in the air like a peacock's fan. She struts. She mugs for the audience. The crowd of gathered families is laughing, egging her on, *lilietsa*-ing along with her.

Now the seal is broken. As other children proceed to the front, their mothers, sisters, aunts, and grandmothers run up behind them, doing hilarious dances, shaking their asses, singing, screaming, waving at their children, shaking their arms in astonished blessing, then staggering back to the rest of the family, bodies sagging under the weight of hilarity and joy. The graduation has become a graduation party. People are openly talking, pointing at these mini adults, hugging them, dancing. And then, as the metaphorical cumulus clouds part, I understand why Nthabeleng wanted us to come.

Tseli was one of the first children Nthabeleng's organization took in, over five years ago now. She was half-dead when they found her. The two former Peace Corps volunteers who founded the safe home—before they recruited Nthabeleng to run it—told me that the squalid hut where Tseli had been abandoned was one of the worst they had ever seen, reeking of shit, death-haunted. Tseli's mother was in jail for burning down the house of a rival. Her father had moved on to another wife in another village. And by the time she graduates from kindergarten, Tseli's mother and father will both be dead, part of a generation of parents and caregivers that AIDS is in the process of reaping.

Tseli Moeletsi died and was resurrected in that hut. There is no good reason that she is alive and thriving today. There is no logical reason she shouldn't be tucked into a tiny grave in the low terraced cemetery by her father's village, with only a small wirework decoration marking the spot. Like so many children before and after, throughout this region, throughout this country, Tseli should be forgotten.

But she is not. She stands before us now, grinning in her too-big robe, amused by Nthabeleng, this madwoman who adopted her, raised her, coaxed her back from the dead. But for the dedication of a few people who turned their home into an orphanage, Tseli would not be here, in this goofy outfit, at this ridiculous ceremony. She is a laughing, knee-scraping, mischief-making slap in the face of despair. She is a rebuke to submission, to giving up, to accepting the inevitable—to the fact that children die all the time in Lesotho.

It is Easter Sunday for Tseli, for Nthabeleng, for all the mothers out here, scores of them standing in this furnace, dressed in colorful *seshoeshoe* dresses, running up to dance behind their children, who receive a diploma that says they have lived to age five, unlike so many siblings and cousins. In the Western world, we feel entitled to our long lives, are aghast that we might not receive our full eighty plus. So many of the women in this crowd have lost three-year-olds, one-year-olds, three-week-olds. Ellen shared the story of a grandmother in one of the outer villages who said that, of her ten grandchildren, six were dead, two were HIV positive, and two were healthy. These are not uncommon numbers. This is the reason for celebrating kindergarten graduations, here and everywhere in the world.

As we walk back toward the safe home, challenging Tseli and her tiny friends to footraces and games of tag, I understand what Nthabeleng wanted to say but never would—that despite all the self-important speechifying and the blistering heat, all she could hear were the words: "Tseli Moeletsi, please come accept your diploma."

JINK

When they ask me, I smile, but actually it's more of a smirk. Outward smile, inward smirk. Maybe they don't realize that English is my first language.

"No, no, join us," they say, after I decline again. "We like to play each day at lunch."

I have started working at the high school, and my new colleagues have already been incredibly welcoming. Ntate Baholo, my direct supervisor, is the head of the Math and Science Department. Ntate Lebo teaches English, Ntate Katleho chemistry, Ntate Makalo civics, Ntate Linkoe and Ntate Pheko computers. These six friendly Basotho men are trying to get me into a midday game of Scrabble.

"It is so important," they tell me, "to refresh the mind during lunchtime."

But I am working through a tricky calculus in my head. My position at the school is tenuous, and the last thing I want is to squander any staff room goodwill. They have taken a significant chance on me: a teacher who has never run a classroom before. I spent the previous year student teaching outside Detroit, but the undertaking was a dubious one; one of my notable achievements came when I located a forgotten faculty-only bathroom where I could sleep-hide during passing periods. Sometimes I was able to attain a position of delicate balance there, leaning up against a ledge with my forehead pressed to the cool tile, where I could briefly forget how very bad I was at my job.

My classroom management skills were, perhaps, underdeveloped. I once watched in amazed horror as one of my students threw a primed rat trap at his best friend. It is unclear to me whether the rat trap was found in the classroom or was brought from home, but either way, not ideal. Jayden, the thrower, was a notorious ladies' man who told me he modeled in his spare time, and I did once catch him surreptitiously circulating an eight-by-ten glossy around the classroom, a picture of him stretched shirtless on a faux tiger rug. Cameron, the throwee, was just over five feet tall and was well known to be the strongest person in the school, who could have bench pressed me if inclined. He showed up to senior prom in a cream white suit, cream white shoes, lavender shirt and tie, and a bejeweled Hello Kitty medallion the size of a grapefruit that hung from his neck. And while I had no control over these boys (I can still see the rat trap frozen in midair, full of potential, as Jayden calmly told Cameron: "Catch."), I did love them in an older-brotherly way. While they spent each school day probing the methods of my psychological downfall, they spent their weekends making YouTube videos where they freestyled over instrumental hip-hop tracks, mostly rapping about food they hoped to consume in the very near future. (One video was a diss track aimed at a Subway employee who had skimped on sandwich toppings.) Whenever they had a video they considered especially good, they would send it to me for adult critique. I think they appreciated the fact that I took their nonsense seriously. This is perhaps my finest attribute: I take all nonsense seriously.

Jayden and Cameron were not alone in testing the dimensions of my authority. (There was none to test, but they persisted anyway.) Toward the end of that year I discovered another one of my favorite students, a girl on the basketball team, sitting in my empty classroom during free period. She was sweaty, her feet up on the desk, wearing only a sports bra and basketball shorts—fresh from a workout, apparently. I walked into the room and immediately turned on my heel to exit.

Separated by a good fifteen feet, we haggled over why I felt it was incredibly important for her to put on a shirt. After a few minutes of negotiation she sighed and said, with a certain bemused exasperation,

"It's okay! I'm not even into guys!" From the hallway, I explained to her that I was happy she felt comfortable talking to me about this, but I was certain my future parole officer would find her logic unpersuasive.

ᛝᛝᛝ

So I am weighing this Scrabble game very carefully. I am eager to leave behind my student-teaching incompetence and introduce myself as a confident and competent ally. I know it will be impolitic for me to begin my tenure here by waltzing into the lunchtime men's club, day one, and beating some asses on the Scrabble board—but these teachers will not let me out of the game, overwhelming me with their polite refusals of my refusal.

"Ah, no," they say, smiling. "It is a must."

Finally I cave, deciding it is worse to seem standoffish. But first I settle on a few personal ground rules: no show-off words; definitely no challenging anyone's words; don't win by too much; get in, get out, have fun, be gracious in victory. Their board is held together with masking tape and the racks for the tiles are all missing. Makalo holds his pieces cupped in his hands. Pheko has his tiles tucked into the slots of a chalkboard eraser. Maybe the word to describe my condition would be *PRE-GLOATING*, which is not an acceptable Scrabble play since it is both hyphenated and non-real.

Then the game begins and these guys start dropping words like *DATUM* and *XYLEM*, not just hitting the words but hitting double- and triple-word scores every time, making two and three horizontal words out of every vertical. Within moments I am trailing by forty points, then eighty. I am flailing. I am undone. This much should have been obvious from the outset.

On one turn, I lay out the word *TREE*. Lebo, who is sitting next to me, notes that I can use my *S* to make it *TREES* and reach a double-word score. I am a charity case.

Then the trash talk starts. Pheko hits a triple-word score and gets "Ah, the wonders of the Lord will never cease" from Katleho. Linkoe lays down a bogus word, gets challenged, and loses his turn—which prompts Baholo to comment: "He has been smote." All trash talk is done in King James English.

Makalo, who is in the lead, puts down the word *MOUV*. Everyone yells, grabbing for the dictionary to challenge, but Makalo laughs and rearranges the letters into *OVUM*. Just keeping everyone on point.

In the meantime, I am able to land the word *TAN*. Three points.

Baholo follows me with *JINK*. Forty points.

But here I am at a crossroads. *JINK* is clearly not a word. After staring at it for a moment, I realize that he is aiming for *JINX*, which would indeed be a strong word. But *K* is not *X* any way you look at it.

Baholo and Makalo are separated by just a few points, and *JINK* boosts Baholo into the lead. Everyone is staring at *JINK*, trying to decide whether to challenge. No one wants to risk forfeiting a turn this late in the game—they are silently calculating this against the possible points they have in hand.

I consider the situation. On the one hand, I had previously decided not to challenge anyone's words. But on the other, I am the only one in a position to truly know whether the word is legit or not. I ask myself, *Is it not my responsibility to see a fair outcome to the game?*

But I chicken out. I let *JINK* slide. Baholo wins and Makalo angrily tosses his remaining tiles onto the board. I have finished in seventh place out of seven: *LAST*, four points.

After he returns the board and tiles to the box, Baholo, my supervisor, puts his arm around me. "My brother," he says—addressing me forever with this same endearment—"My brother, I was so curious to see if anyone would challenge my word."

He is smiling his victorious smile.

"I was so *curious*."

He flips open the dictionary.

"But if they challenged me—*hei!*—they were going to get a surprise."

He is at *H*, then *I*, then *J*.

"They were going to get *hit*"—he is paging through the *J* section—"hit so *hard*."

Then he finds what he is looking for, sitting at the top of the page, first word in the column—JINK: v. intr. *to make a quick evasive turn, to dodge, to change direction abruptly.*

Baholo smiles at me and snaps the dictionary shut.

CALL ME MOSHOESHOE

We have strolled into town this Saturday to watch the conclusion of Lesotho's annual high-altitude marathon, which culminates in a sprint along the wind-whipped main drag through Mokhotlong. Hundreds of townspeople have gathered along the road. As we walk, I consider the logistics involved in running this marathon. The lowest point in Lesotho is 1,400 meters *above* sea level—almost 5,000 feet up—the highest low-point in the world. The elevation here in Mokhotlong District, where I get shortness of breath from chewing too quickly, ranges between 7,000 and 11,000 feet. The runners will be finishing this 26.2-mile race, along these murderous gravel roads, up these rollercoaster grades, with times just over two hours.

We head toward the finish line, scouting for prime spectating locations. Nthabeleng and her sister Kokonyana have joined Ellen and me this morning.

"Hey, Moshoeshoe!" Nthabeleng yells at me. "Get moving or I'm going to watch this race from your shoulders!"

Kokonyana, who works on the NGO's outreach team, begins laughing her giddy round-cheeked laugh. "Yes, yes, Moshoeshoe, you must make haste!"

Both Nthabeleng and Kokonyana delight in addressing me by my Sesotho name. They do it as often as possible, in front of as many people as possible.

ꗾꕫꕡ

If you live in Lesotho for any amount of time, you will acquire a Sesotho name, unless you are unloved or possibly unlovable. Strangers along the road will fall into step beside you and—after inquiring into your business in the country—will inevitably direct the conversation toward your Sesotho name.

"Ah no," they will say, "it is a must. You must take the Sesotho name." They will then suggest an appropriate name. Several strangers suggested I take the name Mpho, which means *gift*, and which is a girl's name.

But perhaps this underscores why Sesotho names are objectively excellent: they literally mean something. Maybe you have heard a new parent declare, "We named him David, which means *beloved*." This is only true if you live in ancient Samaria. In North America, in the present day, David means David. Sesotho names are far more fascinating, however. One boy I know carries the name Lebuajoang, which means "How do you say?"—word for word—*Le bua joang?* Rethabile, a joyous and jowly baby who lived at the safe home for several months, literally means "We are happy"—*Re thabile*—which is something you might declare if Rethabile were your child. As a final example, the Sesotho word for "dog" is *ntja*, the word for "mother of dog" is *mantja*, and Mantja—a delightful woman who works on the outreach team—has parents with distinctly non-Western taste in names.

The point I am trying to make, though, is that I didn't want a girl's name. This is why I asked Nthabeleng to give me a new Sesotho name.

"Something regal," I tell her. "Something befitting my stature."

"*Ache, uena*," she sighs. "You are regal like a *fariki*."

But she plays along. Nthabeleng stares me down for a second, sweeping over me with a coolly analytical eye. "Okay, you can be Moshoeshoe." A pause. "And for the surname, you will take Mochochonono. From now on we can call you Moshoeshoe Mochochonono."

She is grinning now.

"A real Mosotho man."

It becomes clear the following day that there is something unusual about my Sesotho name. When I introduce myself as Moshoeshoe

Mochochonono, the man I am talking with falls off his stool laughing. He is drunk, I should note, and we are in a bar, but still—his reaction suggests some irregularities with my new sobriquet. This is confirmed when I deploy it again and the female bartender yells: "Ah ah—it cannot be!"

When I confront Nthabeleng with these results, she begins shouting. "You said you wanted a regal name, *uena!* Now you are blaming *me?*"

A bit of context for those unfamiliar with southern African history.

Moshoeshoe: founder and first king of Lesotho.

Moshoeshoe: national icon, hero, saint.

Moshoeshoe: person of first-name-only importance, like Oprah or Prince or Jesus.

When I press her on the matter, Nthabeleng admits that the last name was the funniest-sounding surname she could think of on the fly. "For Basotho people, it is too much."

She makes this clear with a demonstration, pursing her lips and gumming over my new name: "MO-SHWAY-SHWAY MO-CHO-CHO-NO-NO! MO-SHWAY-SHWAY MO-CHO-CHO-NO-NO!"

In the United States, it would be something like having the name Georgewashington Humperdinck.

٤.♡.٤

Back at the finish line, we have staked out an excellent vantage point and are chatting with some locals. As they greet people, Nthabeleng and Kokonyana refuse to introduce me by anything other than Moshoeshoe Mochochonono. But I must admit that I have grown fond of my new Sesotho moniker, in part because I have learned that the original Moshoeshoe was a brilliant and charismatic roughneck-savant, the kind of guy you'd get Denzel to play in the movie.

Moshoeshoe came to prominence in the 1820s as a cattle raider, cattle being the ultimate status symbol of southern Africa. Moshoeshoe was so skilled at making cattle disappear from nighttime mountain pastures that people soon began addressing him by the praise name of, well, "Moshoeshoe," which translates roughly as "The Shaver" or "The Razor." Say it out loud—MO-SCHWAY-SCHWAY—and you will understand its onomatopoetic nature. The sound you hear is that of an upstart no-name as he shaves clean the grazing land of rival chiefs, psychologically shearing them of their manhood.

Over several years, as Moshoeshoe accumulated cattle—as well as increased reputation, status, and power—he began to amass that most valuable of natural resources: allies. Neighboring tribes began to willingly offer their allegiance; other local groups fell into conflict, but Moshoeshoe—who always favored the non-violent path—never stepped on vanquished foes and was wise enough to let assimilated chieftains rule over their own people. During his transition from genial highwayman to regional power player, tribal warfare was raging through southern Africa, and Shaka Zulu and his armies had left thousands of families uprooted and wandering. Always a canny strategist, Moshoeshoe offered shelter to these refugees as long as they operated under his brand. In a further act of generosity fused with psychological leveraging, the Razor dipped into his massive bovine war chest and doled out cattle to the refugee families, cattle that essentially became their property. Under this system of *mafisa*, everybody won: the newly moneyed refugees swore their lives to Moshoeshoe and the ranks of the Sotho swelled.

(And while perhaps enough has been said about Moshoeshoe's general decency in a time of political vacuum—which additionally included instituting a system of direct democracy, abolishing the death penalty, and forbidding the cultural practice of killing "witches"—it is also worth noting that he publicly forgave the enemy chief who killed and ritualistically ate Moshoeshoe's own grandfather.)

The man had an innate understanding of human behavior, but his knowledge of the land around him secured his legacy as *Pater Patriae*. As his nation grew, he established his headquarters on a flat-topped mountain that doubled as a natural fortress. This spot offered abundant fresh water, plentiful pastureland, a commanding view over his kingdom, and only a handful of easily defensible mountain passes.

So when the Ndebele, another powerful regional group, decided to take a shot at Moshoeshoe, he crushed them, literally. As the Ndebele doggedly picked their way through the mountain passes, the now-numerous Basotho rolled boulders down on top of them. And then, in a gesture that can only be labeled "Moshoeshoe-ian," he sent a hecatomb of fattened cattle after the retreating Ndebele. It was simultaneously a peace offering and a taunt: "Good game" and "Fuck you." And it was practical too: the limping Ndebele lived off the cattle on their way home, surviving to inflate the myth of the Razor, the man who dropped boulders on them and sent them away with a consolation feast.

At the height of his power, Moshoeshoe even defeated the British, twice. In 1851, the Brits, who had always been looming in the distance, decided it was time to assert their authority over this native rabble-rouser. A soon-to-be-disgraced Major Warden sent a force of one thousand men up the mountain; Moshoeshoe promptly sent them back down again. A year later, a British force of twenty-five hundred arrived, led by a man named Cathcart. They were properly equipped this time and intent on humbling Moshoeshoe in front of any other indigenous troublemakers who might be watching. The British invaders were quite surprised then when Moshoeshoe and his rifle-wielding Basotho cavalry fought them to a standstill—a second very public humiliation for the colonizers.

But Moshoeshoe was a pragmatist, a man who knew his limits. By the mid-1860s, he was starting to lose the total control he had once exercised and he was unsure who his successor would be. Even worse, the Boers—Dutch Calvinist frontiersmen—were chipping away at his territory in increasingly bloody battles. Over the course of just thirty years, Moshoeshoe had coaxed a fragile nation of almost 200,000 people from a handful of decentralized farmers and cattlemen. He wanted to see that nation endure.

The Razor was no bridge-burner; he had left his interactions with the British on honorable terms. After repulsing Cathcart in 1852, Moshoeshoe famously sent a letter declaring Cathcart victorious in his loss, an olive branch that was snatched up by the British. In 1866,

Moshoeshoe reached out with an offer of annexation. The Basotho would voluntarily come under British rule as long as they could maintain a sense of national identity.

In 1868, the British colony of "Basutoland" came into existence. By 1870, Moshoeshoe was dead.

꙳ ꙳ ꙳

I am thinking about my namesake as we stand near the marathon's finish line. I take in our surroundings, this nation that he cultivated. The land is rugged *in extremis,* the ring of peaks across the ravine reaching 8,000 feet, the lone road into town tiptoeing along a gorge where the Senqu River ribbons below. I can almost see the boulders careening down through the valley, can almost hear the armed Sotho galloping through on horseback.

Suddenly the crowd begins to stir. Runners appear on the horizon, out past the edge of town, where a wooden sign requesting *Kena ka khotso* leans against the wind. We push forward, eager to take in the finale of this grand human *agon.* Shepherds rein in their horses and draw alongside. These beasts, with eighty-kilogram sacks of maize meal strapped to their backs, stamp and whinny in the dust. From here the shepherds will continue on to cattle posts further up in the mountains, where they will wait out solitary nights.

In the distance, we hear sirens. Two police motorcycles tear down the road, lights flashing, clearing the course for the leaders, sponsored international athletes testing themselves up here in the clouds. There are two men in full sprint, separated by no more than a foot. The crowd comes awake, living in that symbiotic moment of spectator and athlete, the crowd driving the runners onward. The two men stride, a sheen of sweat on their faces, bound at the hip by an invisible cord. We watch the pulse of muscle, the translation of energy along pavement, the striking ugliness of the human body at its limits. The man in the lead is barely able to maintain his foot of separation as he leans through the finish line. We cheer and clap and we are satisfied in some general way.

But there is a third man back.

No one else is in sight. This man, he cannot compete with the first two. He is clearly a great runner, but he is not a sponsored athlete. He has separated himself and will take third easily, but we can see it—we in the crowd—we understand that he will never win these races.

And then, rather suddenly, the man has competition: not other runners, to be clear, but a pickup truck that has swerved madly into the road behind him, bearing down hard. The truck is close on his heels now, four people in the cab and ten people in back. They are standing and yelling and seem to be urging this nameless runner on.

Kokonyana begins waving her arms, then looks back at us with wide eyes: this man is from Mokhotlong!

"*Tiea! Tiea! Tiea!*" she shouts—"Strength! Strength! Strength!"—as she dashes into the course after him, after the truckload of cheerleaders, laughing as she goes. And Nthabeleng is off after her, bellowing, "*O tla fihla!*"—"Almost there!" The crowd is roaring for their native son, even the impassive shepherds cheering. He will take third!

As I watch him run, I remember a race back in Chicago, a high school cross-country meet where my sister Anne, eight years younger than me, was competing. At Montrose Beach, Lake Michigan sweeps out to the eastern horizon, and just inland there are hundreds of high school runners from across city and state, a giddy throng of hormonal youth navigating the course in heats. Meanwhile, I am staring out at the churning lake, doing my best impression of a Caspar David Friedrich painting: I am a young man contemplating some important matter of metaphysics, in my early twenties and dwelling in whatever solipsistic embrace that implies. Then I catch a glimpse of my teenage sister chugging up the Great Hill, that devious course killer—she is lanky and flushed and working hard, maybe fifteen and somewhere back in the pack—and before I can process how exactly it has happened I find myself at the course ropes, shouting her name. There is no time to consider whether this aligns with my romantic posturing.

"Anne!" I am screaming. "Anne!"—it is all I can think to say—and she passes by with her eyes on the ground, a look around her mouth that is either amusement or annoyance or some blend of the two. I watch her go, surprised to find tears in my eyes.

The man from Mokhotlong passes and the crowd thunders its approval. I can see his face twisted in agony and a strange wave of pride washes through me, a visceral full-body shudder.

I want to reach out to him, I want to call out his name.

VALENTINE'S DAY

On Wednesday, out at the high school, I find an unsigned note in my mailbox. I have just come from teaching my Form D math class where we have been exploring the vibrant mysteries of Venn Diagrams. This is what the note says:

I never knew that ordinary days could bring such happy news until I somehow chose you as my Valentine. Thank you for being a part of my life.

When I read this note aloud in the Math and Science staff room, it elicits howls of laughter from my colleagues. Ntate Baholo, Scrabble victor, and my deskmate 'M'e Poho snatch the dainty epistle away from me, parsing the handwriting and speculating about specific wording.

Poho rereads the last line. *"Thank you for being a part of my life.* Ntate Moshoeshoe, is there something you are not telling us?"

She puts the back of her hand dramatically to her forehead, then begins fanning herself with the handwritten note. "Whatever has transpired, you must hide it from your wife, as she may become murderous."

ᗺ.ᘜ.ᖇ

I show the note to Ellen later that night. She reads it, nodding calmly. As I watch her I am reminded of the time, some years back, when she fought off a bat that attacked us in our sleep. It flew in circles around the ceiling, shrieking, and then dove at us.

I retreated to the corner and huddled, fetal, thinking how darkly apropos this all was—that I should enter the world naked, and now, many years later, exit the world naked, bitten to death by vampire bat. Then I realized that Ellen had, with a certain Canadian equanimity, swatted the bat with a rolled issue of *The New Yorker*, trapped it under a recycling bin, and released it into the wild. It set out briskly for the tree line.

She looked over at me as she returned to bed.

"Are you okay?" she asked.

ﷺ

Thursday, I receive another love note in my school mailbox:

Hi, Honey, You look sick today, did you take too much beans yesterday? I will like to take you to the Hospital. So tell me when you are free. I think you need an appetizer for tomorrow.

This note receives a more sober reception in the staff room. What exactly can this signify: *did you take too much beans yesterday?* Is the writer suggesting that I am flatulent? It seems an odd tactic for a secret admirer. The line that reads *I will like to take you to the Hospital* is perplexing as well—is it seduction or threat? To my American eyes, the hospital is a decidedly unsexy place, but what can I possibly know about the cultural weight of "the Hospital" vis-à-vis Basotho sexual mores?

But it is Valentine's Day tomorrow, and what can one really know about these matters of the heart? The secret notes that I've been receiving are part of the local interpretation of Valentine's Day—something which I'm assuming was originally transmitted via Christian missionary, and which has now been assimilated in the Basotho style, where any common event can become a multi-day celebration. We faculty members have all picked names out of a hat and have been writing secret lurid notes to each other throughout the week, the first sparks of a love that will burn hotly through the school year. Tomorrow is the big reveal: during lunch we will receive gifts and learn the identities of our *innamorati* before the real party begins.

꒰·ღ·꒱

When I asked Ellen if she wanted to get married, I gave her a piece of gummi candy rope that I had tied into a ring-like shape. It was an item I had purchased moments before at a 7-Eleven. She looked at what I was offering and she did not say no.

She put the engagement ring on her finger, sized it up, and ate it.

Only later did she explain her actions: she was worried that she would try to save it otherwise. The gummi ring would grow disgusting, a slowly decaying *memento mori* that had once symbolized eternal love.

As she tells me this, I am picturing her childhood bedroom in Toronto. When she was fourteen, she found a green conjoined triplet gummi bear in a packet of candy, and in a fit of excitement she scotch-taped it beside her bed. It rots there to this day, a thin green stain down the wall beneath it.

꒰·ღ·꒱

Friday has finally come: Valentine's Day, warm and lovely in this southern hemisphere climate. In the staff room, the teachers are abuzz with last-minute speculation about the identities of their valentines. When the lunch bell rings, we crowd around the windows of the Math and Science staff room. Outside, there is singing and ululating.

Here come the members of the Humanities staff room—the teachers of English, Business, Civics, Religion, and Sesotho—dancing in single file and belting out traditional songs in antiphony. They process across the school grounds, fourteen women with gifts in hand, six men singing and marching beside them. We teachers in Math and Science are cheering and urging them on.

Meanwhile, one thousand students have gathered to watch this spectacle. As their teachers march past, they are collapsing in laughter, struck down with joy, splayed out in the dust—casualties on the battlegrounds of *amour*.

꒰·ღ·꒱

Once Ellen and I went to a friend's wedding. Late into the night, she began arm wrestling the partygoers. I had gathered a sizable crowd of mostly strangers and was collecting bets, provoking the challengers, driving up the pot. Ellen bested one woman after another—it wasn't even close.

Soon the men came on. The first one she dispatched quickly, bloodlessly, and he immediately retired from combat. The next man was defeated with equal vigor—yet he kept coming, losing again and again, unable to process this strange new world he had inherited.

I walked the circle and collected dollar bills from chumps. I would have proposed to Ellen right then, had we not already been married for some time.

༄·❦·༄

As the line of shuffle-stomping Basotho arrives, the Math and Science staff room erupts in dancing. A large stereo system has materialized in the corner and is now blasting American hip-hop. Teachers pull me around in unfamiliar steps, the entire faculty united in this midday nightclub. Students peer through the windows and teachers make no attempts at decency.

After a few minutes, someone turns off the music and a large circle forms. Anticipatory silence fills the room. Then one by one, the teachers go to the center of the circle to reveal their hidden identities, each person presenting a final gift and giving a ludicrously flamboyant speech on the excellence of his or her "vallie." Each speech is met with wild applause. Teacher after teacher sends forth a paean to love both earthly and divine.

Now my secret vallie is in the center, a shy male math teacher who has been happily listening to the speculation about my note-writer's identity. He gives me a coffee mug filled with candy and a tentative hug.

༄·❦·༄

We were in Rome when Ellen got pickpocketed. She had gone for the day out to the catacombs, toward the edge of the city, and I had stayed behind to do nothing. She was waiting to buy her ticket when she realized what had just happened, her bag suddenly lighter, then turned immediately and ran, chasing after a departing figure.

She caught them in the parking lot, a standard pickpocket team of three men: one to distract, one to make the snatch, one to receive the handoff. A cloud of dust picked up and rolled across the parking lot, perhaps a tumbleweed too. The men stood staring at her.

"Give me my wallet," Ellen said.

The men yelled and protested their innocence. Ellen took a step forward. They considered this briefly, having never encountered an adrenaline-dazed Canadian in the wild. Then one man threw down the wallet and they ran.

Even those pickpockets knew better than that poor sap at the wedding, even they did not want to end up like the bat.

⌇⌖⌇

The number of speakers is dwindling. I am hanging back, suddenly nervous. But finally there is no one left. People are looking around the room to see if anyone still remains, as one teacher is giftless.

I step inside the circle and clear my throat. I pause for a very long time.

When I begin to speak, my voice is ragged with emotion. "Some of you will know that deep in my heart, in the most secret and passionate corner of my heart, one name is written there."

A murmur of approval shimmers through the room.

"There is one name," I continue, "one name that the angels sing to me while I sleep."

Yes, they are nodding, *preach, my brother*.

"One name written in fiery love."

Amen, my brother, amen.

"That name is dearer than my own. Forever on my lips, it is the name of my vallie."

I pause to wipe an imaginary tear.

"That name is 'M'e Poho."

'M'e Poho: my deskmate, loud and hilarious, a bullish juggernaut of a woman whose barbed tongue is forever lashing ignorant students.

'M'e Poho: who said to me on my first day, looking haughtily down at my lunchtime plate of green legumes, "I see you have pea'd yourself at lunch." She paused appropriately, arched an eyebrow, and added: "Perhaps tomorrow you will beans yourself."

'M'e Poho: rumored to be a powerful consumer of alcohol, a woman who once, when I ran into her at one of the local bars, offered me her daughter—her teenage daughter who was standing shyly beside her—as a "conc," an offer which charted some devilish course between the lands of *serious* and *not*.

'M'e Poho: this giant woman, somewhere in her fifties, screams when I say her name, falls to the floor in a Pentecostal state of ecstasy. She clutches at her heart and her head. She begins crawling across the floor in her nicest *seshoeshoe* dress, moaning with joy, until she reaches me and—taking hold of my ankles—beseeches me to say that this is no dream but reality.

꿈.♡.꿈

I can remember well the circumstances of our first encounter. Ellen and I were at a party thrown by mutual friends and we got to talking. It seems now that our paths were bound to cross eventually. A few days later, I called her up.

"Yeah!" she said happily, "you were the guy in the lumberjack shirt."

"Mmhm," I smiled through the phone, tight-lipped, nodding in case she could somehow see me. I was not the guy in the lumberjack shirt.

But tonight we are walking out along the gorge, watching the sunset soften the jagged clefts of the earth, the falling light now charging the landscape with strange cryptozoological power. Across the river, the hills have taken on the appearance of massive beasts slumped against the land, dozing in Mesozoic slumber—fantastical creatures with thick furred hides, no known kingdom or phylum.

"Hey," Ellen says. "Do you want to have a baby?"

A BRIEF PRIMER ON SOME MATTERS OF ETIQUETTE (AS PRESENTED BY AN OUTSIDER)

Touching

Once I saw two male police officers walking down the main road, holding hands. Uniforms crisp, batons dangling, pistols holstered, fingers linked. They looked fierce, hidden behind mirrored aviators, bonded at the fingertips.

I tell Ellen about these policemen. She tells me she rode in a truck out to a distant village. Two men were squeezed into the front seat beside her, and one placed his hand on the other man's thigh for the duration of the trip. His hand rested there with the casual familiarity of a lover.

Everyone holds hands here. Everyone touches. Men with men, women with women, tough teenage boys with tough teenage boys. It is not uncommon for a stranger to take your hand as he walks beside you, asking where you are going or what has brought you to Lesotho. This type of physical contact can be initially disconcerting, but the beauty of holding a stranger's hand reveals itself gradually on a stroll across town. *Enter with peace. Kena ka khotso.*

Staring

Back when I first arrived, I asked Nthabeleng why everyone was staring at me.

"What do you mean!" she yelled, because there is nothing Nthabeleng hates more than direct questions, and nothing she loves more than yelling. "You are always asking these things. Don't you have eyes or a brain?"

As I turned to leave her office, she yelled after me: "They were probably staring at your pink face!"

The Basotho will stare wherever you go in Mokhotlong. This is fundamental. Men, women, and children, old and young, rich and poor—it doesn't matter. They will stare and stare hard. They will stop what they are doing, they will freeze in mid-conversation, they will get out of their cars to look.

There is no menace in any of this. The reality is simply that people are interested. If you are white and in Mokhotlong, then you are one of maybe twenty white people scattered throughout a district of around 100,000 Basotho, which means your whiteness accounts for 0.02 percent of the district population. Really, though, your whiteness or non-whiteness is only part of the story. You could be Indian; you could be Neptunian. You are simply Not Basotho in a country that is 99.7 percent ethnically homogeneous.

After living in the mountains long enough, a question will wriggle to the surface of your mind. One day you will think: "What's wrong with staring?" You will reconsider that long-held injunction of your childhood and wonder: "Why is it so bad to look?"

Eventually you will embrace the stare. You will bask in it, you will wallow in it. And then you will learn to stare back. You will stare at the taxi drivers who hang halfway out their windows, rolling down the road in slo-mo, bleating quick staccato honks as they troll for customers. You will stare at the Sesotho doctors and their unknowable knots of root and bark, their baggies of pale powder. You will stare at the schoolkids skipping by in their matching greens and whites, matching reds and whites, matching blues. You will stare at the two missionaries from Kansas. You will stare at the cobblers and welders, the ditch diggers and accountants and trash burners. You will stare at the jail guards and government agriculture consultants, the man roasting chicken feet, the grandmother selling dense wheels of steam bread, the barbers, preachers, and butchers.

You will stare at the cattle (the cattle won't stare back, don't care, the dark marbles of their eyes dreaming already). Because aren't you somewhat curious about your fellow planet-goers? Haven't you too experienced the transgressive thrill of locking eyes with a stranger and holding that glance too long?

Feeding

We have nineteen in the minibus already—this vehicle designed for sixteen passengers—when we stop to pick up a mother with two small children along the side of a high mountain pass. It is late. There are no more taxis coming this way tonight.

They slide the door open and the mother passes her nine-month-old baby up to me. I cradle her in my arms while the mother wedges beside me and situates her six-year-old daughter on her lap. We sit slotted like an overstuffed box of crayons, shoulders around our ears, twenty-two riders now. In this posture, I pantomime fatherhood, playing peek-a-boo with the baby nested in my arms, curious to see how this new costume might fit. Eventually, though, the child becomes upset and begins to cry, so to stave off commotion in our hyper-condensed state, the baby's mother unwraps her top, pulls out her breast, and begins to feed the child I am still holding in my arms.

Soon the child relaxes and falls asleep. The mother leaves her breast out of her shirt for the duration of the trip. It is just a few inches from my face and, if so inclined, I too could lean over and sip. I do not.

I must pause for a moment.

We Americans are fearful of nipples. They are terrifying to us, hideous, even. We bundle and conceal and pad them. We airbrush them from lingerie advertisements. We protest and sign petitions against them—they are the Maginot line between a teen-friendly PG-13 and an R rating, that designation of moral bankruptcy. Pop singer Janet Jackson's nipple was famously the source of a $550,000 fine levied by the United States Government, in a case that spanned more than seven prosecutorial years and eventually involved the Supreme Court. Of the nation. These nipples, they are anathema.

Yet we cannot look away from our American breasts. We package them for public display (not the nipple), we revere them in both the still and moving picture. We prop and inflate them, cantilever them over open space. We harness them as our engine of culture, as our national resource, our nuclear future.

I hope it will not be distasteful to suggest that the Basotho have a more measured approach to breasts and nipples. I hope it will be clear that when one of the college-educated employees on the outreach team undid her shirt and began squeezing the excess milk from her engorged postpartum breasts, it was not considered overly shocking. Nor is it considered odd that the women in the clinics don't hurriedly cover themselves after having a breast exam, perhaps in the same way that one does not rush to cover one's elbow after having an elbow exam. Here in Mokhotlong, a breast is a part of the body. A nipple is used to feed children.

In the taxi, people are slowly dropping off. There is still another hour or so before we reach our destination. The baby is drowsing in my arms, the breast close at hand, and the mother looks over at me and smiles. As the taxi jostles along, I see the woman's head nod briefly, then she rests it against my shoulder and falls asleep.

THE GIRL BEHIND THE COUNTER

I know a girl who works at the local butcher shop. I suppose I shouldn't say girl, since Limpho is a woman, probably in her middle twenties. But the urge remains. She has a gentleness that makes her seem younger than her years, some bruiseable quality, although she surely knows more of the roughness of life than most. She works in a hog butchery, after all, a barn-like structure humming with bellicose and predatory horseflies that patrol the blood-freckled floor and swoop aggressively in while you eat your meal. It is one of my favorite places in town.

The Thia-La-La butchery is one of Mokhotlong's premier noon hotspots—is in fact Mokhotlong's only noon hotspot. Midday at Thia-La-La involves a chaotic press toward the lunch counter, a Soviet-style food rush as the hungry masses of the eastern mountains shove their way forward. They wave for attention and slam money on the counter, while the staff responds with a whirlwind of inactivity, since it is not the Basotho way to rush. Some days—as you press slowly forward, as you observe the glacial preparation of a meal, as an employee scoops chips onto a plate, one by one by one by one, forever and ever amen—some days you feel the clammy embrace of madness closing in around the backs of your ears. It is a singular sensation and thus worth experiencing at least once.

Today, though, I am able to catch Limpho's eye across the counter. She is attending to someone's plate with soul-withering fastidiousness, positioning each of the *makoenya* like she's preparing a Dutch still life—each fat cake in its rightful place—but when she sees me she abandons her opus and adds more chips to the deep fryer; she knows I like them crispy-crispy.

I know all the staff now, heading toward the end of my first season in Mokhotlong: 'M'e Makatleho is a jovial chit-chatter; Ntate Motlatsi will gladly discuss the merits and demerits of a footballer like Cristiano Ronaldo. But I am especially drawn to Limpho. There is something jarring about seeing her behind the counter, against a gory backdrop of hocks and shanks, steaming coils of intestine, a metal tray of purple-pink chicken hearts arrayed like a row of penis tips, when Limpho looks so much more like a librarian.

Limpho the hog-butchering librarian skips behind the counter as she works, sometimes singing, always smiling. The rest of the staff loves her too, perpetually floating jokey chastisements or lighthearted flirtations her way. I talk with Limpho when I can, at least as much as my weak Sesotho and her weak English allow, but Limpho's fan club is legion and everyone must wait their turn.

૭.ⱱ.૬

Ellen is telling me about her research as we stroll through town. She had been out at one of the clinics the previous day, where she works closely with the nursing staff. Often she observes clinical practices and talks with the nurses about how HIV is treated in these far rural zones, but occasionally Ellen herself is pressed into duty if the clinic is especially understaffed—all hands on deck.

Yesterday a man came in toward closing time, Ellen says, brought his wife and small child with him. He was nervous and pacing, clearly uncomfortable. The wife was unsure what they were doing there. She didn't understand that the man had come for an ART appointment—antiretroviral therapy—and had brought them along as a way of disclosing his HIV-positive status to them. He had been doing this for months now, coming to the clinic in secret, sneaking around to take his meds, some strange form of infidelity.

Ellen and I duck into Thia-La-La for a moment, dodging the sun, and wave to Limpho as we enter. She heads for the deep fryer, then places a bottle of vinegar on the counter before I can ask. While we wait for the chips to fry, Ellen continues her story.

Out at the clinic, the woman was beginning to comprehend her husband's revelation. She and the child entered an exam room to be tested by the HIV counselor, a government-paid specialist who was trying to head home for the day. The test showed they were both positive.

Later, a nurse went to check on the mother and child and discovered that the HIV counselor had administered the test and then left them in the exam room, had not in fact counseled them on anything—what this diagnosis meant, what their treatment would look like, how their daily routines would alter—*ache!* it was closing time, after all. The mother and child didn't even realize they had been abandoned, didn't know they were owed an explanation, had sat there waiting patiently for someone who had clocked out and left.

The nurse talked them through their situation, tried to explain how things were about to change. Then, as the mother and child exited the exam room, they found that the husband too had slipped out, unable to bear the scene. The clinic was empty.

꣼꣼꣼

Sometimes I visit the butchery in the late afternoon, once the lunch rush is finished. Seating at Thia-La-La consists of four small communal tables with wooden benches, where you sit shoulder to shoulder with wind-blasted shepherds or crumpled grandmothers or the men who work on power lines. Sometimes you sit beside the town's lone madman: eyes wild, beard matted, clothed in plastic bags. These tables are intended to seat two on each side, but—as with many things in Lesotho—maximum capacity is treated as a loose guideline or perhaps a dare.

I am reading as I eat my meal, a practice that initially raised eyebrows—this public reading—but which has come to be accepted as the slightly cracked behavior of a harmless knucklehead. I pull from the cold glass of a Fanta bottle. I crunch chips well crisped and doused in paprika and vinegar. I leave greasy fingerprints on the pages of my book. Limpho is behind the counter, humming to herself as she gaily shears off hunks of gristled mutton.

Many afternoons pass like this, surrendered to deep comfort.

⁂✿⁃

It happens quickly.

Ellen and I have been in South Africa for several weeks, rambling through Bloemfontein and Cape Town. Then, shortly after returning to Mokhotlong, I head into the butchery to say hello and find Limpho in disturbing health.

While she has always been thin, I am shocked to see her suddenly gaunt. She must have been steadily losing weight for some time, but the change is stark after a long absence. And while Limpho frequently wears a woolen winter hat, as many Basotho do even in warm weather, she has now taken to wearing layers of heavy sweaters under her blood-spattered apron.

Soon Limpho is not gaunt but wasted, her health bending exponentially in the wrong direction. When I come in the following week, she can barely walk across the room, her face drawn, her eyes absent their color.

I say hello and she gives me a wan smile and heads to the back room.

And then Limpho is gone, taken off to the hospital in the interior district of Thaba-Tseka.

"Closer to her village," Motlatsi tells me. "She will return when she is healthy."

Not long after this, Motlatsi himself takes a new job forty-five minutes away, through the mountains, in the town of Mapholaneng. New employees come to Thia-La-La, unfamiliar faces. Occasionally I ask them if Limpho is getting any better, but the new staff don't know who she is.

୬୯ୣ

One day I come into the butchery to discover that a grand leap in culinary technology has occurred. Thia-La-La now features soft-serve ice cream, *ex nihilo*, non-dairy manna delivered from the heavens. The clientele is abuzz but hesitant. The owner of the butchery has made a wild investment in the machine; he has heard they sell this soft-serve in Maseru, in the capital city, and he intends to revolutionize the palates of the deep countryside. But other butchery-goers are wary, the crumpled grandmothers and the men who work on power lines looking cockeyed at the strange churning contraption. The owner is struggling to recoup his money, but I take the cause on as my own, a personal mission to underwrite the machine four *maloti* at a time.

I am in ordering soft-serve one afternoon when I notice that Motlatsi is back from Mapholaneng, a happy surprise. He has come into town for the day to cover someone's shift. As he hands me my chocolate-vanilla swirl, he says without preface: "She is gone."

I don't understand him properly at first.

"She is home?" I say. "She has gone home from the hospital?"

Motlatsi nods his head.

"That's great. Is she coming back to work here?"

Motlatsi looks confused. Then he repeats it. "She is gone."

I stare dumbly, then walk home with my ice cream melting in the sun.

୬୯ୣ

This is the last thing Limpho says to me.

It is Friday and we are walking across town for dinner, Ellen and Nthabeleng and I. In Mokhotlong, there is nothing more beautiful than this: walking leisurely in the early evening, through that amber glaze, passing men and women on the road, sometimes fellow teachers, schoolchildren too—all of us with the shared knowledge that the working week is done. People laugh with their neighbors, line-drying laundry gusts in the darkening air, kids race handmade toy cars down the hill, men drink along the road. Every third person stops to talk with Nthabeleng, since she is the boss in town and people must show obeisance. Ellen chases after some children she knows and they scream with delight.

Across the gorge, we can see dark torrents of rain moving inexorably toward us. The setting sun lights up the storm clouds with gaudy, spectacular color. Rainbows span the entire breadth of town, and up ahead that familiar sign: *Kena ka khotso.*

A white pickup speeds past us, then stops in the road.

It reverses to where we are walking. An arm is beckoning to me.

I walk over to the window. It is two men from the butchery, with Limpho between them. She leans over and puts her hand on the window. "I am leaving," she says. "I am going to the hospital." The two men look straight ahead.

Limpho—her name means *gifts.*

"You're sick?" I ask, as if I do not know.

"I want to say goodbye."

"I'm sure I'll see you again soon," I tell her. What else could I say?

Limpho smiles and does not reply. The truck heads off for Thaba-Tseka.

II.

SUMMER

WE EAT, WE DRINK, WE DANCE

We went with Nthabeleng out to Matsoaing, the village where she grew up, a cluster of rondavels settled at the base of a valley. A flat shallow river ran along the valley floor and women were drying blankets on the rocks. We had come to honor the fifth anniversary of her father's death.

I sat with the men in a loose circle and we passed around a large cup of homebrewed joala, each taking a few sips and then sending it along. The women were beside us, stoking the cookfire, where a heavy black cauldron of sheep viscera bubbled; occasionally they would step into the circle and sip joala too. Neighbors wandered by, stopped to talk for a moment, sipped the joala, then moved along to other business or stayed and joined the circle. The cookfire smoldered and washed over us like a beekeeper's calming smoke; we felt happy and stoned in the summer breeze.

When the viscera were done cooking, the women ladled stew into a red plastic washbasin, and this too was passed around the circle. The cooking of the sheep would come later—this was the afternoon snack. We plucked out small bites of intestine, lung, trachea, heart, tripe, and reserved the liver for the women. When the pieces were gone, we passed the basin again and sipped broth: rich and fatty and well seasoned. The afternoon drifted along like this in gorgeous fashion. Our only responsibility was to sit together and share some food and drink.

Years before, I had worked at a homeless shelter in Phoenix, Arizona. The man who ran the place was a Catholic priest, and each morning he would open up the parking lot of the building and celebrate mass outside.

Some benches were arranged under a shade tent and we would gather there, staff members like me, or suburban volunteers, or people who had slept outside—junkies coming off hard nights, old women who talked to themselves, people who just wanted to get out of the sun for a while. When it was time for Communion, the priest would bless a tortilla and pass it around the group on a plate; when it reached you, you tore off a small piece if you wanted, then passed it along to the next person. It was hard not to notice the way the food bound us—addicts and priest and affluent volunteers and drifting college grad—hard not to be aware of the way we had all just shared the same substance.

In Matsoaing, the warm afternoon breeze swept over us. A dog lay comatose in the shade by the cookfire. I watched the cups pass around the circle, watched the celebration build gradually, while people told stories about Nthabeleng's father.

It was a bridge.

PARTY CRASHING, OR
THE KINGDOM OF LESOTHO

As I walk into the Math and Science staff room, there is a serious argument underway. Several teachers are present—some prepping for their next class, some sleeping, some eating, some listening in—but it is Ntate Pheko and Ntate Linkoe, from the Scrabble club, who are at philosophical loggerheads. Both men are in their mid-twenties, both are charming and funny, and both would probably rather be doing anything other than teaching at this rural high school.

I am quickly appealed to as an impartial arbiter. The conversation transitions from Sesotho into English.

Linkoe addresses me first. "Ntate Moshoeshoe, this man—*hei!*—he is so stubborn. He is saying that when we have a party for teachers here, it is improper to invite outside guests to that party."

"Yes, there should be no outside guests," Pheko breaks in.

"But this man!" Linkoe shouts in exasperation. "I am saying, when outside people are having a party, then even Ntate Pheko wants to be invited. But when the teachers are hosting a party, then he does not want the outside guests to come."

I nod at the equitable nature of Linkoe's point.

"It is somehow hypocritical," he says, closing his argument.

I nod again.

Now Pheko addresses me. "But you see, Ntate Moshoeshoe, this man is not telling you all that has happened previously."

I ask what has happened previously.

"It was too much! At the last party held by the teachers, two outside guests arrived. And one of these outside guests pointed his revolver at a teacher."

I indicate that this does seem relevant as well.

Another teacher helps me piece together what happened at the last staff party. These two outside men, who were brought as guests, partook heavily from the teachers' stash of alcohol. As the party continued, with bottles of beer and bowls of trail mix moving in circles through the room, the outside guests' overconsumption came to be seen as a violation of etiquette. Eventually one teacher—running on adrenaline fumes and homebrew—confronted the outside guests, claiming they were stealing beer and stowing it in their backpacks.

A demand from the crowd was put forth to see the interior of the backpacks. One outside guest opened his backpack, removed a pistol, pressed it up against the bridge of the teacher's nose, and informed him that he was now holding in his hand the total contents of the backpack.

None of the teachers thought it prudent to mention that there were several stolen quarts of beer in view.

So while I consider the facts before me, understanding that Linkoe has staked claim to a moralistic perspective—*Invite Unto Others As You So Wish To Be Invited*—I also understand Pheko's utilitarian perspective, which argues that the least number of teachers should be shot in the face.

I tell them I can see both positions clearly and that both positions have merit. But before I can deliver my verdict, Pheko interrupts:

"Ntate Moshoeshoe, there is one last reason for not inviting the outside guests."

Pheko is an excellent storyteller—he has a great yarn about the time he was repeatedly almost struck by lightning while heading out to sleep with a woman in another village—and he knows his way around a pregnant pause. He is snickering now as he considers how to word his next remark. A few of the other teachers are smirking now too, familiar with the story he's about to tell. Even Linkoe, whose position seems to have been reasonably rebutted by the *Let's Not Get Shot* counterargument, is suppressing a smile.

"*Kannete*, Ntate Moshoeshoe, *kannete*. You see, one of the female teachers at the party became very interested in the other outside guest, the man without the pistol."

Muffled laughter around the staff room.

"Yes, she became too interested in that man."

Pheko is in full raconteur mode now, pacing around the room.

"And she gave that man a gift."

He is unsuccessfully trying to retain a dignified and lawyerly tone.

"But it was not a gift given to the teachers. She gave that gift only to the outside guest."

Open laughter now.

"And I am asking, is it right then, is it proper, to give a gift to the outside guest alone and not to the fellow teachers? The ones for whom the party existed in the first place?"

My deskmate, 'M'e Poho—my vallie and great partner in staff room hijinks—addresses me calmly: "Ntate Moshoeshoe, do you want to know what that gift was?"

But Pheko will not be beaten to his own punch line. "She gave him Lesotho!" he yells, and the staff room collectively loses it. One of the younger female teachers pulls her sweater over her face, blushing madly at such loose talk. Poho is hooting with joy and shaking me by the arm.

"She gave that man Lesotho!" Pheko yells again, in case he has not yet made clear this most excellent Sesotho double entendre.

"You know what Lesotho is?" Poho asks me. "Lesotho is where we all come from!"

"Lesotho," Pheko repeats, "the place that men love so dearly!"

'M'e Buang chimes in with feigned earnestness: "You know, Ntate Moshoeshoe, this Lesotho—it is a very small place."

"Yes," 'M'e Kananelo says, "Lesotho is a place where the road goes between the bushes."

"Ntate Moshoeshoe," 'M'e Mosa asks me, "did you know that Lesotho is a land of so much water? *Kannete*, it is true!"

Even Linkoe joins in: "Yes, this Lesotho has a deep valley."

To which Pheko adds: "Yes, deeeeeep, deep dongas in Lesotho."

"Such a beautiful garden, this Lesotho!" Poho calls out, still clasping me by the arm.

Throughout the day, my colleagues continue to drop pun after fantastically juvenile pun. They reel them off, then pace themselves—waiting for a moment when everyone seems to be finally hard at work again, or until just after a student has left the room—then goad each other into further improbable feats of innuendo brinksmanship. It is one of those lovely moments in which the best response is simply to lean back in your chair and bask in the oneness of humankind. I feel deeply honored that these teachers have recognized me as a fellow traveler along the lanes of the lowbrow, the alleyways of the absurd, the pathways of the perverse. And I am rather looking forward to the next teachers' party.

A VISIT TO THE WHITEHOUSE

I am walking out toward the airport that doesn't exist, pondering weighty topics like Cloudking. This is where I do my heaviest mental lifting, out here along the gorge, where the rock falls away into frigid river, where the blue opens up like a hymnal. The land is green and blooming, full summer coming on fast, and this brilliant cloudless day reminds me of the time I briefly lost my mind.

I lost it because there were no more clouds. They were gone—vanished, banished, *nebula non grata*—weeks like this. The eye groped as the perfect blue flattened into mathematical abstraction. Azure unending.

When had I last seen a cloud, anyway? I began to panic.

Blank weeks rolled by. I kept a cloud journal, each page as empty as the empty sky. I had never so much as blinked at a cirrocumulus or a nimbostratus before, but as the barren days stretched on, the cloudvoid took on devastating proportions. It felt anticipatory; it was a clearing-out, a making-room-for, an announcement of _____. The ceiling of the world yawned in mocking midrange blue.

Then one day.

I was walking along the gorge—heading to the Whitehouse just as I am this very minute—when I turned to look back toward our rondavel, sensing a presence. A darkness crept over the surface of the mountain, engulfing shrub and gulley, plunging shepherd and flock into gloom and swallowing our hut. Deliberate and sentient and enormous.

Cloudking.

It was a month of missing clouds, a condensation confederation. This object, this entity, this impossibly massive *thing* drifted overhead with staid and grandmotherly dignity. I stood gaping. I bathed in its shadow. It eased across the empyrean like a sky-whale from a child's fantasy novel. Then it slipped over the rim of mountains and was gone. I felt shaky and baptismal. I may have wept, it's hard to say. Cloudking, this epic poof, restored balance to the world.

༄༺༒

The Whitehouse is a bar—the very bar, in fact, where I introduced myself as Moshoeshoe Mochochonono and a man's brain short-circuited. The Whitehouse sits forlornly in a field of ankle-high vegetation, a sweeping scrubby flat, squatting out here in self-imposed exile because it used to be an airport. This was before Mokhotlong realized it didn't need an airport.

Even the word "airport" is misleading. The Whitehouse is a single low building in a field. There are no terminals or baggage claims, no loading zones or security fondlings. There is just a house—white—and a piece of flatness, the only flatness around, making this flatness *de facto* the airport. The control tower stands a hundred yards off, only one and a half stories high, as if shrunk by a miniaturizing ray. In the distance hangs an orange windsock, limp and humiliated. As Papa Hemingway once said, it looks like the flag of permanent defeat.

At some point, a crafty entrepreneur realized that although Mokhotlong doesn't need a fully functioning airport—there's maybe one arrival per day, the occasional helicopter bearing supplies for the LDF, or the infrequent Piper Cub flown in by missionaries—it can always use another bar. Thus, the Whitehouse.

Or, to put it another way: all airports have bars, but this bar has an airport.

༄༺༒

As I approach the Whitehouse, I can hear the soft pop of gunfire coming from the LDF base across the gorge. The Lesotho Defense Force, the country's army and air support, has a tiny outpost on a remote plateau across the river, unreachable save through a single gated entrance. The base languishes in perpetual gray inactivity, having penetrated my awareness only through occasional gentle reports from target practice. Up here, these sons of Moshoeshoe prepare to rebuff whoever it is that might need rebuffing.

Today there is a car parked out in the field in front of the Whitehouse, its four doors flung open. Three men are holding quarts of beer and dancing beside the car, blasting a single song on repeat. The hip-hop singer Akon, whose voice is tinny and Auto-Tuned, is plaintively declaring—

I wanna make love right now, na na.

I wanna make love right now, na na.

—which seems reasonable.

I head inside and secure a quart of Redd's, a type of South African beer that tastes like apple juice. It is for women only. Many months later I will take a tour of the facility that produces Redd's and will discover, in its promotional material, that Redd's is "for the hard-working woman who deserves time out" and, additionally, "for the woman who likes to showcase her vibrant, vivacious side." I am guilty of both.

This afternoon Ellen is off interviewing some local religious leaders about their perception of the AIDS crisis. I have been wandering about town, happy to be purposeless, and have come this way specifically seeking the mellow Whitehouse vibe. The bar is sleepy most days and today is no different: a weary unloved couch, some plastic lawn chairs, a bored young barmaid leaning against the counter. Will it be a cliché to report that a ceiling fan turns lazily overhead? But it does. The revolutionary languor of this fan is nonpareil.

The scarred snooker table is currently occupied by the bar's only customer: a mother lining up her next shot, her one-year-old daughter wrapped *pepa*-style to her back. The child's head, shoulders, and arms poke over the top of a blanket that swaddles her to her mother. As the mother thrusts her cue sharply forward, the child tilts precariously side to side like a bronco buster in the saddle. When the mother leans over the balding green baize to eyeball a tough angle, it seems the child will be ejected onto the table, but she remains astride and unflappable. The child stares me down with blasé, beautiful eyes. Across the room, the barmaid has fallen asleep, her cheek on the counter.

I take my Redd's outside and settle into a white plastic chair under the eaves. The three men are still drinking and dancing to Akon, the mountains spraddled righteously behind them. I laze and savor the moment, then take out my book of Hemingway short stories. The cloudless sky offers no respite from the noon sun. It will be cold after sundown, but for now my shirt is sticking in patches to my chest and a delightfully warm gauze has drifted down over my field of vision. The beer is cool and my responsibilities are minimal. I start to read but quickly abandon the undertaking. At this moment, Papa Hemingway's words are the verbal equivalent of a hard-knuckled noogie to the crown of the head, unpleasant horseplay from a gruff uncle.

Then, in my periphery, I notice that the three dancers have been joined by a fourth man, a soldier in an LDF uniform, and they are assembling a gun of some kind, which the soldier has pulled from an olive rucksack.

Let it be noted that I see guns in Mokhotlong all the time. Policemen with pistols stroll down the main road. Soldiers with ancient carbines guard the post office. Two men with rifles once sauntered into the safe home to collect back wages for a fired employee, while the children stared saucer-eyed at the jackbooted goons in their playroom. Even the Chinese-run grocery store hires a Mosotho with a pump-action shotgun to stalk the aisles, discouraging theft. I have never shoplifted once.

Over the course of its short national history, Lesotho, which gained independence in 1966, has seen every shade of putsch, coup, attempted coup, military ouster, constitutional suspension, contested election, and state of emergency—many of them prominently involving the Lesotho Defense Force. And while elections from 2002 to 2012 were generally peaceful and democratic, another attempted military coup in

2014 resulted in political upheaval after LDF soldiers opened fire on Prime Minister Tom Thabane's security detail and forced the PM to flee into South Africa for a week.

But as I observe these four men from under the brim of my baseball cap, considering whether or not to abandon my post, I realize there is something slightly off about this rifle. Even a non-expert in firearms like me can see that the proportions are wrong. Then I realize it is a BB gun.

The LDF soldier appears to be off duty, or at least I hope he is off duty, for he is already supremely drunk. From his rucksack—his shooting kit, I suppose—he also produces an old metal pitcher, which he places in the low vegetation as a target. It is the kind of metal pitcher you might pour lemonade from if you were at your grandmother's garden party, or which you might pour gin martinis from if you were a character in a John Cheever short story. The four men pull heavily on their beers as they prepare for sharpshooting practice.

The soldier assumes a relaxed stance thirty yards off from the pitcher. Even though it is more or less a toy, he handles the gun with a fluidity that speaks to an intimate relationship with weapons. The three dancers hang back. The soldier exhales and then pops off several quick shots—*ting! ting! ting!*—against the target. Easy.

As he moves to pass the BB gun on to another man, the soldier quickly draws a bead on the man who comes forward. The man yelps in surprise and ducks away. The soldier laughs, clucking his tongue at his friend's sheepishness, and then surrenders the gun. He hands it stock first to the next marksman, then stares off toward the target and emits a tiny dart of spittle from between his teeth.

The other three are clearly amateurs. They giggle nervously as they shoot, mostly missing, occasionally notching a lucky hit, strutting when they do so. The soldier steps into the rotation intermittently. He is smaller than the other men, wiry and filled with lithe confidence, his movements perhaps lubricated by his drunkenness. He does not miss.

Even from my perch under the eaves of the Whitehouse, I can hear the BBs leaving the rifle with impressive velocity, a high whine. After a few rounds, the soldier goes to retrieve the target, examining his handiwork. The pitcher is dented and pockmarked from the metal pellets. This prompts a single repeating comment from Akon.

The men continue drinking and shooting. The day blazes on, but the heat of the sun is suddenly interleaved with chill slashes of wind feinting and juking across the field.

And then I find myself up with these men, fitting the stock of the rifle against my shoulder. It is not entirely clear to me how this has occurred—some form of apple beer–infused participatory journalism, which perhaps is the only kind worth doing.

"You must aim it just so," one of the amateurs is instructing me.

"Yes, yes, careful," another one says.

The soldier cracks open the chamber. He is rationing his BBs now, dishing them out one by one. He digs into his pocket and pulls out a single metal pellet.

"Here is your bullet," he says, holding my gaze. "Now you must kill the man."

I roll the BB around in my palm. It is an insidious little shard of metal, silent and jagged.

"Yes," I say. "I will kill that man."

I line up the pitcher and ease my finger onto the trigger. The sun is disorienting and bright in my face and there is beaded sweat at my temple. A passage from *The Stranger* pops into my head—that icy, lifeless book—but I shoo it away.

I take a breath, then pull the trigger. The bullet *whangs* out of the barrel and touches nothing.

The three dancers laugh and slap me on the back. The soldier takes the rifle away from me and says, in a voice flatter than the surrounding field, that I have failed to kill the man. He reloads the gun and *tinks* and *tanks* the pitcher several more times, as if I might somehow absorb his skill.

And then, quite casually, as a bird passes low overhead, the soldier pivots smoothly and picks the bird out of flight with a single bullet. The bird dips off, then falls awkwardly from the sky and flutters into the brush. The three dancers fall silent.

The soldier smiles at us.

I can see the bird shuddering in the scrub vegetation behind him.

It is at this point that I decide—well, perhaps I shall be taking my leave of these fine gentlemen, and needless to say it has been such a pleasant afternoon, and how very courteous of them to include me in the fun, but really I am running late just now for a standing engagement, and would they be so kind as to excuse me, with the enduring hope that we all meet again soon?

I ease back toward the white plastic chair where my belongings sit, turning repeatedly to wave and smile, feeling distinctly uncomfortable with my back turned. As I collect my bag, I can see, from the corner of my eye, the soldier again genially menacing his friends, leveling the rifle at them as they duck and howl, their voices a curious blend of complaint and fear.

And yes, occasionally he pulls the trigger and little plumes of dirt geyser around their feet, and they are now yelling with a bit more urgency in their voices, cut it out, seriously, that sour note of fear beginning to predominate. But I am walking back through the field and heading home fast, the sky blue as blue overhead, hoping for Cloudking.

ス.ぴ.ᔑ

A postscript:

Unrelated, maybe. There is no way I can ever prove it, since I don't know what his name was. Maybe it's just a thing that happened.

"Hey," Nthabeleng asks me one day, "did you hear about the LDF base?"

We are sitting in her office, debriefing at the end of the day.

"Some soldier, some crazy—he killed his friends out there."

She shakes her head, wondering.

"He came into the barracks in the night and shot them while they were sleeping. They had some argument, I guess. Three men, just dreaming away, then *bang! bang! bang!* and that was the end of them. They said the soldier was very drunk when he did it."

Nthabeleng sighs, looks at me, then looks out the window.

"What can you even do?"

A BRIEF PRIMER ON THE SESOTHO LANGUAGE (AS PRESENTED BY A NON-SPEAKER)

Human-Doughnut Grammar

Sesotho, the language of the Basotho people, is a captivating and complex idiom. Not only does it provide the non-speaker with such exotic delights as "pops"—written either as the letters *q* or *qh*—but it smashes consonants together in pleasingly non-Western fashion, resulting in verbal pile-ups on the expressways of the tongue. Consider, for example, words like *ntlhoea* (they hate me), *qhaqholotse* (to pull down), and *hlahlobile* (to examine).

To a student of the language, perhaps the most challenging aspect of Sesotho is the concept of noun classes. Nouns fall into seven classes, and each class has a different way of showing singular and plural. Unlike English, which generally denotes singular and plural at the end of a word—*book* and *books*—Sesotho takes care of this business up front. One native of Lesotho is a **Mo**sotho, whereas a whole group of locals are **Ba**sotho. One person is a **mo**tho, several people are **ba**tho.

A word's noun class is not arbitrary. Any Sesotho grammar book will tell you that nouns related to human beings are generally grouped together (with **mo-** as the singular and **ba-** as the plural). Additionally, nouns related to animals fall into a different category (**n-** and **lin-**), nouns related to abstract concepts are situated together (**bo-** and **ma-**), and nouns describing physical objects are cordoned off accordingly (**le-** and **ma-**). This brief summary is by necessity a simplification, as concepts like "the law of nasal permutation" are likely outside the purview of the casual reader. I will also acknowledge that reading about grammar is possibly dull, and for that I offer an insincere apology.

Here is my point: the word for "white person"—*lekhooa*—falls not into a *human* noun class but a *thing* noun class. The singular and plural of "white person"—*le*khooa and *ma*khooa—is shown in the same way as the singular and plural of "doughnut"—*le*koenya and *ma*koenya. Before we proceed, I should note that these *makoenya*, deep-fried dough balls of local specialty, are delicious.

When I first noticed this—*lekhooa* being a word that any white person in remote parts of Lesotho hears constantly, where children excitedly scream it across fields and from the tops of jagged promontories—I assumed I had made some rookie linguistic error. This is a prospect that remains likely. However, I soon noticed that this "thing" designation pertains not only to white people, but to any outsiders. Chinese immigrants are called *le*-China and *ma*-China. Albino people receive the somewhat derogatory labels *le*soefe and *ma*soefe. The same goes for *le*kwerekwere and *ma*kwerekwere, words that southern Africans use (often mockingly) to describe Africans from the north. When I pointed this out to Ntate Baholo in the staff room one day, demanding that the Zimbabwean teacher Ntate Gappah and I be granted full personhood under the Sesotho language, he assured me that I was mistaken. There was no malice or insult intended in our non-human classification.

Surely this is correct in the practical and daily application of the word *lekhooa*. It just means "white person." I am confident that the Basotho do not really see outsiders as *things* rather than *human beings*. But language is often more powerful than we are willing to acknowledge. The words we use color our perception of reality in subtle ways. This is the Sapir-Whorf hypothesis, an idea—formulated in the 1930s, fallen out of academic favor by the 1960s, semi-resurgent since the 1990s, and now co-opted by me, a non-anthropologist, non-scientist trying to make a probably fallacious comment on grammatical minutiae— which states that the specific words we utter have actual effects on our cognition. *The language we speak affects our perception of reality.*

Studies in this realm, known in the journals as "linguistic relativity," have shown that the language a person speaks can actually affect how that person perceives specific colors, distances, and spatial relationships—things that are objectively *fixed* and non-negotiable.

So would hardcore Sapir-Whorfians argue, as I jokingly suggested to Baholo, that Sesotho does ever so slightly dehumanize people of non-Sotho origin, linking them subconsciously to inanimate objects, to things like doughnuts? I don't know, but I should stop before I spin completely out of control. In fact, I don't even think "hardcore Sapir-Whorfians" exist. And while the Sapir-Whorf hypothesis is intriguing in general, I can't buy into any version of it that actually impinges on free will or leans toward determinism. No self-respecting scholar would claim that our thoughts are *controlled* by the language we speak.

My point is simpler, I suppose: our words are always charged just beneath the surface, our vocabulary freighted with personal history, half-remembered conversations, and forgotten inside jokes. Our lexicon is perpetually infused with a strange brew of the personal, the political, the emotional, and the spiritual. And in the end, I am proud to share a noun class with *makoenya*. Would that all human beings were as crispy and satisfying.

What We Talk About When We Talk About Food

I am eating lunch with the other teachers one day when I make an innocent comment to 'M'e Mosa. "Your cookie," I tell her in my cobbled-together Sesotho, "looks very nice."

Mosa blushes and Ntate Baholo rushes to my assistance. "Ntate Moshoeshoe," he says, "my brother, there are some things that it is not possible to say as you have said. You cannot talk about 'M'e Mosa's *cookie*, but only her *cookies*, using the plural."

"Yes," my deskmate 'M'e Poho says, elbowing me and gesticulating in a way that would get one fired in some workplaces, "because with her cookie, you are talking about something else entirely."

Ntate Pheko, who was almost hit by lightning, enters into the conversation. "In the same way, Ntate Moshoeshoe, you cannot comment upon Ntate Baholo's carrot—only his carrots—or else people will become confused with your meaning."

"No, no," Poho agrees, "you should never discuss Ntate Baholo's carrot, nor the length of his carrot, although it is appropriate to say that Ntate Baholo has sizable carrots growing in his garden."

Mosa, having now finished her cookie, adds: "Yes, and in a manner relating to what 'M'e Poho has said, you should not inquire about the potatoes of either Ntate Baholo or Ntate Pheko."

"And you must certainly not ask which man has more nourishing potatoes," Poho adds.

Baholo is laughing, but nervously, and wishes to steer the discussion away from his carrot and potatoes. "As a final warning, my brother, I should tell you about the cake of 'M'e Mosa, or even of 'M'e Poho. You should never say *Ke batla kuku*, which means *I must have her cake*, even if the cake of 'M'e Mosa or 'M'e Poho looks particularly pleasing. A comment like that may seem troublesome to those who hear it."

The conversation continues in a similarly informative manner, but I must interrupt here to raise this question: why is food the dominant and cross-cultural metaphor for the human genitalia? While the Sesotho language provides "carrot," "potato," "cookie," and "cake"—among many others—we see this in English in abundance, for men ("nuts," "wiener," "sausage") and women (including variations on the words "taco" and "pie," as well as a ghastly phrase involving the words "roast beef"). The male metaphor continues in Italian (*piselli*—peas), Czech (*vejce*—eggs), German (*spaetzle, eier*—noodle, eggs), Russian (*khren*—horseradish), Korean (*gochu*—chili pepper), and Spanish (*polla*—chicken). I am sure a dedicated linguaphile could compile an even more expansive list.

What is the nature of this comestible-genital relationship? Is it due to some basic life-giving quality that both share? Does it indicate that these are the two primary drives in the human experience—food and sex—and that the two are fused somewhere deep in our collective lizard brain? I won't even venture a guess. My task is simply to pose these questions of lasting import, with the hope that our scientists, philosophers, and theologians will carve out answers for future generations.

Language of Love

During my time in Lesotho, I have met a handful of Christian missionaries. These missionaries spend the better part of a year living in Mokhotlong or some other district camptown, learning the Sesotho language, and observing local customs before they head deep into the mountains, sometimes for years. I met one young woman who was setting out for an area reachable only by helicopter. She told me she was prepared to never see her family back in Colorado again.

Somewhere along the way, I obtained a Sesotho phrase book that these missionaries often use to teach each other the language. This book is called *Puisano*, which means *Conversation*, and is printed by the Morija Sesuto Book Depot. The copy I have is the twenty-fourth printing, from 2005. I am going to reprint some passages here, verbatim, and I will try to avoid any editorializing. These dialogues, translated into both English and Sesotho, are imagined conversations that you, the missionary, might have with a local:

"Going to Church" (p. 13–14)

Missionary: Are you coming with me to church? Don't you know that this is the Lord's Day?

Local: Yes, I know; but it doesn't matter. I am not a Christian.

Missionary: Do you never go to church?

Local: I never go.

Missionary: Does your father never go?

Local: Sometimes he goes.

Missionary: Come, let us go together to church.

Local: What shall I go for?

Missionary: You shall go to hear about God.

Local: No, I shall not go. How can you prove that all that is said about God is true?

Missionary: Is it not God who has made all things we see?

Local: How can I know that He has made them?

Missionary: Who do you say has made them? Have they made themselves?

Local: I don't know; I don't care for these things.

Missionary: But you will die, and then go to the judgment.

Local: You Christians say so; I am not convinced of it. I shall go where my forefathers have gone.

Missionary: Do you know where they have gone?

Local: No, I don't. Goodbye; I am going home.

Missionary: Oh no, let us go together to church!

Local: I don't care to go, as I am not satisfied with what Christians are; their conduct shocks me.

Missionary: Do all of them disgust you?

Local: No, I know some who don't.

Missionary: If so, judge by their deeds.

Local: Well, you have persuaded me; let us go to church.

"Death" (p. 19)

Local: I have lost two children. One was a boy, the other was a girl.

Missionary: Were they already grown up?

Local: No, they were still small.

Missionary: Where were they buried?

Local: They were buried in the cemetery, where all the dead of our village are buried.

Missionary: Is it a place surrounded with a wall, and planted with trees?

Local: No, there is nothing, as the Basotho don't take much care of the graves of their dead.

Missionary: Is that true?

Local: Yes, it is true.

"Night, Light" (p. 21-22)

Missionary: In former times, how did the Basotho produce light, when they had no candles or lamps?

Local: They made a light with a piece of fat in a broken pot.

Missionary: Was the house well lit?

Local: Not at all; such a light was of very little use.

Missionary: What did people do in the evenings?

Local: They used to light a fire and sit round it.

Missionary: Did they sit up late in this way at night?

Local: No, they went to bed early like the fowls.

Missionary: How could they sleep comfortably when the huts were so small?

Local: Don't you know that all the boys of the village used to sleep in one hut, and so did the girls?

Missionary: How was it possible in such circumstances for parents to bring up their children?

Local: It was very difficult, because that custom of not living together destroyed the love which ought to have existed between parents and children. Do the Christians still follow this custom?

Missionary: No, the Christians generally build larger houses in which the children sleep in separate rooms.

ꑭꑴꑫ

Sometimes I wonder whatever became of that young missionary from Colorado. She was small and beautiful and had golden ringlets of hair. I would see her along the main road from time to time, when she was on her way to study Sesotho. In my head I referred to her as Goldilocks, perhaps uncharitably.

Once we invited her to a dinner party we were hosting. In the common rondavel, we sat in a circle and passed around bowls of *papa* and *moroho*, quartered chickens, bottles of beer. We played ridiculous games, told fantastic lies. As with any gathering where more than a few Basotho are in attendance, this dinner party quickly became a dance party. The speakers blasted *famo* into the summer night and we stomped around the rondavel, but the missionary would not join us in the dance. She sat off in a chair, polite and distant, her golden ringlets shaking gently in refusal. "You are all too drunk," she told us, but it was not true—we were just too happy, far out along the bridge.

That was the last time I saw her. Sometimes I wonder how she fared out there, far past the shepherds' *kraals*. Perhaps she is still out there, or perhaps she has returned home. I don't think I will ever know.

Before she left, she took the Sesotho name *Lerato*—which means *Love*—and then headed deep into the mountains. Even now I sometimes think to myself: *Where has Love gone? Where can Love be found?*

MIDNIGHT BASOTHO
DANCE PARTY

We are drawn by the pulsing *famo* beat—drawn from our rondavel in dark of night, down past the turn in the river and the semi-deserted hospital, toward the grounds of the vacant hotel and into the gutted adjacent building—some defunct abattoir—where all hog-butchering has been laid aside to give the band some space to play. The building is a dusty cinderblock warehouse, windows painted over, walls shedding plaster, haunted and forbidding.

And there is an honest-to-God *famo* band napalming the stage—actually, there's no stage, defunct abattoirs don't have stages—but the singer is raging and the drummer is raging and the dancers are raging, not the accordionist or bassist, though, because those two stone-faced motherfuckers are motionless, wearing sunglasses, chain-smoking, sitting with their backs to the crowd, and laying down an absolutely dirty line of accordion-bass polyphony.

But perhaps I am getting ahead of myself. I don't want to skip over the man with the machine gun, and I want to make sure, first of all, that we know what *famo* is.

(For the curious: it's **FAH-MOO**.)

Famo, the reigning musical genre in the Kingdom of Lesotho, sounds like some southern African step-cousin of zydeco. The music is filled with plaintive, reedy accordion runs built over a foundation of stuttering bassline and thumping *basso* kick drum, then filigreed with bright guitar flourishes and fluttering synthesizer trills. These last two instruments—the guitar and synthesizer—are unnecessarily rococo additions; accordion, bass, and drums will suffice. Layered over this three-piece shuffle-stomp, the vocals take the form of: A) breathless Sesotho raps, the words all fused into one Germanically constructed superstring, or B) melodic moans that follow along with the accordion line. It is, perhaps, an acquired taste.

But when there is a live *famo* band playing in a warehouse that doubles as a slasher-film backdrop, then one must go, even when it is late and one is in one's pajamas and the man at the door is casually shoulder-slung with heavy firepower. Live music is incredibly rare up here in the eastern mountains of Mokhotlong.

To be precise, the man with the machine gun is not the *first* person to meet us at the door. The first people we meet at the door are collecting cover for the band and they try to jack up the price for us. But then, as we are haggling, the man with the machine gun comes over and ends the bargaining process. We will pay the same price that everyone else did, he says, and not the quoted price, which was double that.

"*Kea leboha, ntate,*" I say, giving him the tripartite Sesotho handshake, because it is always important to show gratitude to the man with the machine gun.

The band is burning through their set. The singer wails into the mic and flops onto the ground, his lyrics beyond distorted through the blown-out PA. The drummer bludgeons his kit until a cymbal stand topples over. His bass drum keeps sliding out from under his right foot, metal supports slipping over smooth concrete, even though the drum is held in place with several small boulders. An unsecured cymbal flips off and rolls away after a particularly vicious crash hit, and an audience member returns it to him. The accordionist is busy not caring and the bass player is busy not caring while at the same time slathering his dirty-dirty bassline all over the floor. The dancers—because the presence of a dance team is another *famo* fundamental—are three men in matching T-shirts, wrapped in traditional woolen Basotho blankets, doing coordinated hop-skips, shoulder-dips, and one-footers, all the while swinging their wooden *molamo* in beer-dazed ecstasy. These are people deep in their *métier*.

Here in the warehouse-barn-abattoir, the crowd is deep Basotho. Everyone is in blankets and gumboots, all the dudes are *molamo*-wielding shepherds, everybody is straight-up *country*. While Mokhotlong camptown is quite rural, it is the district hub and thus modernized to an extent. (Point: there is an ATM in Mokhotlong. Counterpoint: the people withdrawing money from the ATM often arrive on horseback.) The people in the crowd tonight are distinctly not modernized. They are grizzled and backwoods, in from the outer villages where they don't run power lines. Everybody is staring hard at us, unflinching.

That is, until Reid gets up to dance.

Reid—my copilot on the hunt for Rapitsoe the mechanic—and his wife, Bridget, both work for Nthabeleng's organization. So when Reid gets up to dance, borrowing my wooden *molamo*—an intricately decorated shepherd's cane that was made for me by a friend, which I brought along because that is what you bring to a *famo* concert—well, when Reid gets up to dance, people are no longer just staring but bug-eyed and leg-slapping, hooting and ululating. The crowd is jaw-dropped at the fact that this *lekhooa* is not only dancing, and with a legit *molamo*, but this *lekhooa* actually seems to know the steps.

This is because we practice.

Any remaining semblance of propriety is hauled into the street and shot. Soon we are all jammed together on the dance floor, doing the hop-skip and the shoulder-dip and the one-footer, doing the scoot-scoot and the double-stomp and the clackety-hop. The locals are doing the tooth-whistle and the bird-whoop too, since Basotho are—by birthright—the most creative and dexterous of whistlers. This acrobatic whistling is another *famo* essential and is beyond the capabilities of any *lekhooa*.

The dancing goes on for some time. At one point, I split off from a wild pseudo conga line and head to the adjoining public bar to grab some quarts of beer. While I am waiting to pay, a man sitting at the bar asks me: "Are you a promoter?"

I glance toward the warehouse-barn-abattoir, then back at the man on the stool. I tell him that I am not a music promoter, although I am enjoying the band.

He arches an eyebrow. "I think you are a promoter."

I raise my beers toward him and head back to the music, nodding at the man with the machine gun as I enter. We pass the bottles down our row of folding chairs, throughout our group, then send them along to other rows and off into the night.

A short while later, I am talking to the man with the machine gun, casting sidelong glances at his weapon. Since my trip to the Whitehouse, I have become a bit more skittish around heavy ordnance, especially after the three soldiers were murdered at the LDF base.

"My name is Adam," he tells me, using an English name he would have received in primary school. "I am the first man." He grins broadly at his joke.

I tell him I am happy that he is here with his machine gun to make sure no trouble happens at the concert. Adam the First Man becomes bashful, eyes down, seems deeply honored by this remark.

The *famo* band continues to rattle the painted-over windows. The dancers whirligig across the cement floor. One little shepherd boy is out here, maybe eight years old and up well past his bedtime. He is in full pastoral regalia—a blanket worn cape-like over the shoulders, gumboots, wool hat—and he is hop-scotching and drinking from a giant glass Coke bottle, while everyone else is drinking Maluti or Marzen Gold.

Two youngish *bo-'m'e* are sitting in the chairs in front of us. These women are laughing with us, or at us, or both, saying it's fantastic that we know the dance steps and how to hold the *molamo* properly. Occasionally they grab the *molamo* and run off to dance with it—a move which is slightly transgressive, since only *bo-ntate* are supposed to dance with the *molamo*.

After a while, Adam the First Man comes up to me and whispers in my ear.

"Those *bo-'m'e*, you must limit your interactions with them."

He is holding his gun casually, like a walking stick. I look up at him, then over at the women dancing with the *molamo*.

He nods. I nod back.

A few minutes later, Adam the First Man comes back and whispers in my ear again.

"It is okay to talk with them, but you must limit your interactions with them."

I nod again. I tell him that perhaps we will talk with these *bo-'m'e*, but we will limit our interactions with them. I have no idea what this means.

Adam the First Man is satisfied and returns to guard the door.

Eventually—after we have danced a bit more, shown off our shoulder-shaking, our ululating, our *molamo*-swinging—we decide it is time to head back home. We have been doing our best to talk with the *bo-'m'e*, who seem perfectly nice, while continuing to limit our interactions with them. As we head toward the door, the lead singer abandons his microphone to see us out, pumping our hands vigorously, and the band plays on without him. Adam the First Man salutes us, military sendoff, and asks to swap email addresses. We head into the night sweaty and smoky and bell-rung.

In the icy Mokhotlong air, the devil dogs are scavenging: glinting eyes and shadowy profiles slipping serpentine between rondavels. The moon burns with neon intensity, glazing the milky road and lighting our way home. All throughout the night, accordions and cymbals echo from the mountaintops, infiltrating our dreams, an electric lullaby for all the beasts who slumber.

KILLING A PIG

It begins with a party, as things often do.

"We will slaughter a pig," someone says.

Since we have been living in Lesotho—nearly two seasons now, the summer days growing shorter—we have overseen the slaughter of two sheep for two different parties, one of which was Nthabeleng's birthday. We decide it is time to expand beyond quotidian matters like ovine butchery into the more exotic realms of pig death.

In Mokhotlong, the celebratory consumption of meat is a matter of real gravitas, since most people are unable to afford it with any regularity. They derive their protein instead from the humdrum bean and the lowly egg. At a party, though, it is understood that the host will provide meat—usually mutton—a matter of long-standing tradition and personal pride. The scent of animal flesh wafts even from the invitation. "You must come," I can recall Ntate Baholo telling me once. "My brother, we will be eating meat there."

About ten days out from the party, I tell some teachers about our plan.

"A pig?" 'M'e Poho says. "Ah no, I don't eat that one. The *fariki* I think is too dirty."

Baholo objects. "No, this is not accurate. The *fariki* is a fine animal. The flesh is very rich in flavor. It is excellent for consumption—but perhaps only for men."

Poho shudders and sticks out her tongue. "I can attend the party," she says, "but maybe I will take just the *papa* and *moroho* to eat."

❧❧❧

I suppose I should mention that I begin most school days by visiting the swine.

The high school where I teach is part working farm, since everything in Lesotho is part working farm. Hired shepherds graze school-owned cattle through the academic grounds. There are battered chicken coops behind the Math and Science staff room and careful plots of *moroho* out by the volleyball net. But it is the pigsty—down by the rim of the gorge—that I find most alluring.

The pigs tiptoe daintily through their muck-filled stone-and-mortar enclosures, the ends of their snouts tilting, sniffing, expanding, contracting, trying to fathom my purpose there. Some piglets lie massed in piles, asleep and grunting in the shade, dreaming porcine dreams—fantasies of mud and maize husks and more sleep. Beside the pigsty, dung is piled in great iridescent mounds, bejeweled with blue bottle flies, shimmering in the heat.

Anyone who professes to find pigs adorable has probably never seen a pig up close. Or perhaps they are familiar with the manicured pigs that celebrities sometimes own, ironic and calculatedly quirky pets far removed from rural farm swine. Pigs are foul, stinking, rather disagreeable creatures. They are not adorable. They are coarse and bristling with all manner of whisker, tails twitching neurotically. Horseflies skitter in and out of their enormous flopping bat ears, which are a pale, unpleasant pink, encrusted with brittle mustard-colored scabs. Some of the swine have dark ink blotches spotted across their tapered snouts, the same hue as long-faded tattoos.

It is their eyes, though, that are most remarkable: human eyes, guarded by blond, decidedly human eyelashes.

When I come down to the pigsty for my daily visit, the animals scrabble to their feet, emitting warning grunts to their penmates as they splash from murky puddles. They sniff the air to garner information, eyeing me warily before eventually growing accustomed to my presence.

I understand now why Homer sang of the witch Circe, who transformed Odysseus's men into swine. As the pigs watch me expectantly, I am looking into human eyes encased in animal bodies, alive with some frightened, mute intelligence.

☙❦☙

We are four days away from the party. My wife and her brother, Dan, head off to find the requisite pig. Her brother is in Lesotho to visit; he is an experienced chef and thus a good candidate for pig sourcing. Ellen and Dan set off for the outlying villages, further into the mountains, along with 'M'e Matello, a friend who will help negotiate the pig purchase.

The three of them take the pickup out past Linakaneng clinic, past the carapace of a long-abandoned truck that rusts halfway down the valley. They meander toward a village where Matello thinks they can find a pig dealer. On the road, they come across some shepherd boys—jauntily whipping their cattle into rank and file—who point them to a nearby village.

It is a beautiful day and the swine are grazing on the hillside. They are robust, dynamic creatures, these mountain pigs. After Matello haggles with the pig dealer, who eventually settles for the equivalent of $40, they go to collect their new animal. But the pig is uninterested in captivity and immediately bolts for the horizon, bounding off with surprising vigor and agility.

The better part of an hour passes in hot pursuit.

Eventually Ellen, Dan, and Matello—with the assistance of the pig dealer and a pack of harassing dogs—are able to corral the wayward hog. The pig dealer, in a nimble feat of legerdemain, snatches the beast's hind leg as they converge. He upends it and has the animal bound around the hooves before it can react. The pig pants and squirms on the ground, hog-tied.

Now, as they traverse the pseudo-roads of the district, heading back toward Mokhotlong camptown, Ellen hears a thump from the bed of the pickup. She glances to the side mirror, where she can see that the pig, having somehow freed its feet from the rope, has thrown itself over the side of the truck. Matello stops the vehicle.

The pig is dangling over the side of the pickup, still bound around the neck, hooves churning in the air as it is slowly strangled. It looks for all the world like an attempted suicide.

꒰ঌ৴

For three days, the pig lives behind our hut on the grounds of the safe home, tied to a stake we have hammered into the earth. We feed the pig pans of milk and apples. We do not know if this is appropriate pig food, but—our theory goes—this will enhance the animal's flavor. Enlightened gastrophiles are always holding forth on what the animal ate before they ate the animal.

Was it grass-fed? Grain-fed—how gauche! We imagine telling people about this experience, years later, at some exclusive cocktail party.

Of course it was free range, I chuckle, *there's no other way in Mokhotlong. And pan-fed,* Ellen adds. *Pans of cream and apples.*

Nthabeleng's daughter, Tseli, and her friends come by to play with the pig. They think this is fantastic, this pig we have. It is their friend. Children passing on the road are fascinated as well. "Hello!" the bold ones yell as they pass. "Who is the owner of that pig?" When I tell them it is our pig, they begin to laugh. "No, tell us!" they say. "Tell us!"

The pig escapes several times each day. It defeats square knots and bowlines, sheet bends and clove hitches, arbor knots, nail knots, slipknots. This pig is the Harry Houdini of pigs. Sometimes we observe the moment of emancipation and chase after the pig, pursuing it around the fenced-in grounds of the orphanage. Sometimes we go to feed it and find it gone. One time I find the pig sitting behind our hut, having yet again untied itself. The end of the rope lies several feet away, cast off disdainfully. The pig is staring at the mountains as it lolls in the shade. It looks over at me and snorts, eyes showing only disappointment in being paired with an adversary so inept.

One midnight I step out behind our hut to urinate. The night is perfect black, soundless, and holy. Nearby, the pig begins snoring sweetly, and I consider going to pet it, but I stop myself—no one wants to be woken from a dream about flying.

ᔑ.ᔑ.ᔑ

Today is the day we kill the pig.

Here comes Senkatana, riding majestically onto the grounds of the safe home, looking like some southern African Hercules. He is tall, muscular, and bearded, wrapped in what appears to be an animal skin. He is wearing the weathered bucket hat that shepherds favor, with his tattered gray pants tucked into his gumboots. Senkatana dismounts from his horse—whipping his animal-skin cape back over his shoulder—and laughs. This laugh is not triggered by anything in particular, but rather indicates the great pleasure he takes in existing. His laugh has the timbre of a baritone sax, oozing mellowed virility and relaxed confidence. It is honeyed and warm in a way that is impossible to fabricate.

This man, Senkatana, is the ur-Mosotho. Nthabeleng has suggested we hire him to do the actual slaughtering, based on the rather sound assumption that if we are unable to keep a pig tied to a stake, we cannot be trusted to oversee its humane execution.

It is perhaps relevant to note that any Mosotho man can kill a sheep. In Mokhotlong, sheep butchery is a skill acquired through osmosis, swallowed in gulps from mountain streams and inhaled through the nostrils. During the last party we threw, the man who hacked open the sternum and eviscerated the sheep was a social worker from the safe home. Many of the male teachers I know can do the same.

But the killing of a pig is a different matter altogether. As Senkatana leaps down from his horse, as he unsheathes his colossal knife, I can see the other men staring at him with some mixture of admiration and jealousy. People are milling eagerly now, staff from the safe home as well as various strangers who have stopped in the road to watch. It is a Friday afternoon and some men have begun drinking. The air is charged with anticipation.

It happens like this:

When Senkatana comes around behind our hut, and not some idiot *lekhooa*, the pig knows that the moment of his death has arrived. I can see the flash of instantaneous comprehension. He springs to his feet—and in that tragic instant realizes he has not undone this last rope. Then Senkatana is leading him away squealing, while he tears the earth with his hooves. He is a large animal, as high as my mid-thigh, and it takes three of us to drag him over to the kill zone. Someone has already dug the hole in the ground into which he will pour his blood.

The two sheep killings I witnessed were quiet, almost banal affairs. The sheep went gently to their deaths, oddly mute, without any obvious attachment to life. They knelt—dull-eyed, motionless, docile—and offered up their throats. They lay down, emptying, perhaps gave a last twitch. All of this provoked in me the most bizarre and inappropriate of reactions: anger. What thing lacks the basic ability to fear its own death?

But the pig.

The pig is bucking wildly, all muscle now. Eventually they have him by the fetlocks and flopped over onto his side and bound around the feet again. He thrashes frantically, writhing against the inevitability of this last moment, squealing. Two men hold down his rear while Senkatana kneels on his head, pressing the pig's face into the gravel.

I catch one last glimpse of those frightened *Homo sapiens* eyes behind delicate blond eyelashes. Then Senkatana pulls the pig's head quickly back and makes a deep lateral slash across his throat. The neck is thick with muscle and it takes even the expert Senkatana two more deep slices before the gouts of arterial blood come pulsing forth. This whole time the pig has been screaming in the most distinctly human way. And now, as the vocal cords are cut and the neck opens up and begins to separate away from the body, I realize that the sounds are no longer coming from the pig's mouth, but are issuing directly from the trachea—a pathetic wheezing and gurgling as the carotid artery chugs away over this last spastic vacuuming of breath.

Senkatana gives another sharp upward tug and snaps the pig's neck. The convulsive struggles of the body taper off, the horrific choking sound fades, and the pig is dead. Blood runs into the hole in the ground. All of this has taken about forty-five seconds.

♊.♉.♋

Some logistics:

After the pig is dead, two things occur. The second thing that occurs is the depilation of the pig, the removal of the dense wiry hair that covers its body. This is done by pouring buckets of boiling water over the carcass, then scraping vigorously with the jagged tops of metal cans. Senkatana and his assistants scrub away with these makeshift tools until the pig is stunningly pale and hairless.

But the first thing that happens after the pig's death is the removal of its testicles. These have been promised to Senkatana as part of his fee. With the deftness of a surgeon, he makes quick, artful incisions and then removes the testicles, each of which is bigger than a man's closed fist, perhaps the size of a large mango. He places them on a table—his prize— these two purple, perfect veined ellipsoids. They look like human hearts.

The gathered crowd has turned festive, anticipating the real celebration tomorrow. Men are now grilling the freshly excised organs for late afternoon snacking: heart, lungs, liver, kidneys. Senkatana begins dancing merrily, a quart of beer in hand, and it is only now that I notice he is wearing a black and blue argyle sweater, perhaps from an old J.Crew catalogue. Somehow it works perfectly with the rest of his ensemble: animal-skin cape, gumboots and tattered pants, shepherd's hat and whip, and an argyle J.Crew number from Fall '99.

Even when slaughtering an animal, one must dress to impress.

♊.♉.♋

It is Saturday noon, the day of the party. We have stayed up all night, slow-cooking the pig over a bed of low coals, hand-turning the beast on a jury-rigged metal spit.

Now the women come dancing up from the safe home, in procession toward the pig buffet, their red plastic plates held out before them. They are doing the slow shuffle-stomp and singing a song of thanksgiving as they march. These are the house mothers—the *bo-'m'e*—who care for the orphaned children day and night. The men are eating already, drinking and laughing and leaning casually up against things in the way that all men at parties must do.

Everyone is here: Nthabeleng and her children, Neo and Tseli, the organization's entire thirty-person staff, fifteen teachers from the high school, assorted friends from around Mokhotlong. Also in attendance are a Peace Corps volunteer from New Jersey; two Congolese doctors who give preferential treatment to the children at the safe home; a Zimbabwean teaching colleague of mine and his cousins; a French-speaking Quebecer on a six-month furlough from her job; and a wind-blown British woman hiking her way through Lesotho, whom I found wandering in town earlier today and looking rather hungry.

People begin to dig into the hog. The *bo-'m'e* pile their dishes high. Tseli razes small towers of meat in a way that American five-year-olds cannot. The teachers, through mouthfuls, argue the relative merits of spit-roasting versus grilling. The night watch—Ntate Bokang and the ancient Ntate Motsi, who alternate nights shivering next to a small fire in the guard shack—are giddily tearing through platefuls of pork. Motsi is—*can that really be?*—Motsi is dancing as he eats, Motsi who is older than Jesus, older than the oceans.

The meat is unlike anything I have eaten before. It does not taste like milk or apples. It tastes feral and unsubtle. Is it possible for meat to taste vigorous? This meat tastes vigorous.

We eat, we drink, we dance. Someone has run miles of extension cord up from the safe home and the *famo* blasting from the speakers sounds like an explosion at the old accordion factory. Everyone is joyously shake-shaking, even the kids, up from the safety of the building, in our arms now and laughing maniacally at this adult madness. Now someone is passing the charred head of the pig around. Its face is frozen in a warlike snarl, lips pulled back to expose jagged teeth. This quickly becomes a photo op. The teachers pose with the animal's head, proof that they ate pig at some crazy *makhooa* party. Bokang the night guard poses with it, pretending to punch the hideous death mask, conqueror and vanquished. Nthabeleng poses with it, holding it in front of her face, ferocious four-foot pig-woman.

As the afternoon stretches, we approach a moment of decadence and comfort which is hard to properly convey. We all dance and shimmy. We sing and stomp. We lie in the grass.

When night comes, we sit around a fire and watch the riot of galaxies overhead.

A PARTIAL DICTIONARY
OF FOOD & DRINK

Boroso: This is the word for sausage; it refers to any seasoned meat mélange that has been packed into intestinal casing. I have often seen men rinsing out the intestines in the aftermath of an animal slaughter, a simple process that involves inserting a garden hose into one end and flushing out unwanted elements.

The first time I eat *boroso* is at a party thrown by the teachers on the last day before a break. We have been drinking in the afternoon out among the deserted school buildings, and by nightfall a general clamor for meat arises.

Inside the Math and Science staff room, the women are dancing to American hip-hop, while outside we men gather around the grill. A cold wind is blowing down the plateau and into the gorge, the first sign that autumn is coming. As we stand huffing in the wind, Ntate Baholo lays an enormous length of *boroso* onto the grill, coiling it carefully as it sizzles and pops. We warm ourselves against the fire, huddling closer, breath steaming like cattle. When the *boroso* is finished, Baholo cuts it into segments to be distributed to the crowd inside. The party has already been a success—no pistols—and I do not think it is an exaggeration to say that, at this point in the evening, the *boroso* is a revelation.

In the darkness, I watch Baholo separate several links onto a different plate.

"Who are those for?"

"Ah, my brother, this *boroso* must be for the night watchman here at the school grounds. I can bring it to him so he will not assault us."

I consider his words for a moment, wondering if perhaps something has been lost in translation. Baholo sees my puzzled look.

"My brother, it is not that he will assault us—"

He stares down into the black void of the gorge and then pulls from his bottle. "But I am saying that these are his grounds at this time."

I nod, feeling that I understand his meaning in some roundabout way, and Baholo heads off into the dark with the steaming plate of *boroso*.

Chakalaka: This tomato-based vegetable curry is often served with *papa* (see below) and *moroho* (see below). It usually consists of diced onions, tomatoes, garlic, peppers, carrots, cauliflower, beans, squash, chilies, and sweet corn. Regardless of ingredients, it is a pleasing word to say.

In Mokhotlong, we buy cans of KOO brand chakalaka, which carries the tagline "KOO: It's the best you can do"—a motto that always strikes me as a tad fatalistic. Buck up, KOO brand products, that attitude is bringing everyone down.

Coca-Cola: Ubiquitous in Lesotho. It may well be the national beverage. Head up to the loneliest mountain aerie and you will undoubtedly run across that iconic red and white. The government has trouble transporting and supplying antiretroviral medications to some of these remote mountain clinics, but Coke? No problem.

Granadilla Twist: Comes in a clear glass bottle with no information other than the word *Schweppes* printed on the container. No product name, no label, just a liter of unmarked pale orange liquid. I didn't even learn its real name until much later, since most people around here just call it "SCHWE-pees." When I first tried it, I was expecting some generic orange-flavored soda pop. What I received instead was a liter of the soda pop that the angels drink in heaven. One day I plan on looking up what exactly a granadilla is, but—you know what?—I will probably never do that. It is better not to know everything.

The flavor of Granadilla Twist exists on a spectrum somewhere between orange, apricot, and peach, with an additional tang in the finish that saves it from over-sweetness. In addition to the clear glass liter bottle, Granadilla Twist also comes in a confusing smaller size, sold in an opaque purple can. Purple does not taste like orange and peach and apricot. Back to work, design team.

Hamburger: Not what you are expecting. Order a hamburger at the Thia-La-La butchery and you get a sandwich of buttery grilled Texas Toast around ground beef pressed so atomically thin that you can see the whirring of valence electrons. This meat wisp is slathered with orange cheeze and ensconced in warm mayo, the end result being shamefully delicious. But order a hamburger across town at the empty Senqu Hotel and an entirely different experience awaits: a recently unfrozen patty, shipped from South Africa, garnished with cold cheese slices, diced pineapple, a thick slab of cold spam, dead tomato, and a noble crown of fried egg.

Iron Brew: Again, I don't know exactly what Iron Brew is, but what a fantastic name. There should be an exclamation point after it. This soft drink tastes like Dr. Pepper mixed with Big League Chew bubblegum. To its credit, it does not taste like iron.

One time I bought the most expensive can of Iron Brew ever sold. Ellen and I were in Maseru, fueling up at a gas station. A refrigerated beverage cooler stood outside, so alluring on a hot day. Through the cooler door, a can of Iron Brew sang to me in a strange and lilting falsetto, and I informed the gas station attendant of my desire.

"No problem," the attendant says. "Only one problem. The cooler is locked and the keys are lost." As I turn to leave, the attendant stops me. "No, no," he says. "We will break the cooler open."

I tell him this will not be necessary. Then another gas station attendant appears; he too believes the cooler should be opened with force. I protest once more, out of courtesy, but these men have made up their minds.

"We will just have to do it at some point," the first man says.

So we proceed to beat the shit out of the lock on that cooler door. One of the men finds a screwdriver inside and the four of us take turns stabbing at the locking mechanism, but the lock is more stalwart than anticipated.

"Wait!" Ellen says, rummaging through her bag. With a flourish, she removes her Leatherman Super Tool 300, an item given to Canadians at birth. *This will do the trick*, we all think.

It does not do the trick. The Leatherman Super Tool 300 breaks almost immediately. The pliers snap clean off. Consequently, the Leatherman Corporation will be receiving a strongly worded letter, as well as a request for a new Leatherman Super Tool 300, unless there is a specific clause voiding the warranty due to instances of breaking and entering.

Disheartened by the broken Leatherman and the unbroken lock, we resort to desperation and animal rage. There is no turning back— the lock is still engaged but now mangled, and no key will ever turn in it again. We take turns beating the lock with the butt end of the screwdriver and the now-defunct Leatherman Super Tool 300, going through a four-person rotation as our arms get tired.

Suddenly the lock goes *click*. Out comes the Iron Brew, the best I've ever had, at a total cost of: one (1) hardened-steel padlock @ 101R + one (1) deluxe Leatherman Super Tool 300 @ 473R + one (1) can of Iron Brew brand soda pop @ 5R = 579R (at conversion rate of 1R = 0.14 USD) = $79.75, plus tax.

Joala: Basotho homebrew, discussed in depth later; decidedly not for cowards.

Makoenya: Deep-fried dough balls, sometimes referred to as fat cakes. Best when purchased fresh from the ladies who sit deep in their *makoenya* lair—that weathered tent behind the taxi rank, their patchy plastic tarp propped up with tree branches, where the hot stink of cooking oil billows out into the day. Roll while still hot in a light dusting of cinnamon and sugar, and only then will you know Beauty.

Moroho: A general term for leafy greens that have been chopped, sautéed, and seasoned; a common component of the Basotho meal, often served with *papa* (see below).

Nama ea nku: This is the Sesotho name for "mutton," which itself is the English name for "elderly lamb." Mutton can be purchased at the Thia-La-La butchery, where the meat is run through a band saw. The result is random mutton chunks—some of pure meat, some laced with dense gristle, some with intricate configurations of bone shard to navigate—all generally delicious. The band saw approach to meat preparation creates an unusual effect: each bite of mutton is a game of chance, to be met with anticipation and some caution; it restrains the chewer from plowing mindlessly through a meal. This is positive in that it teaches the virtues of patience and awareness, and negative in that I prefer my food does not shame me with didactic moral lessons.

The best mutton in town comes from MP Kitchen, which is a tiny metal shack that vanished once. Restaurants come and go, but rarely does an entire structure disappear without notice, and even more rarely does the same structure reappear the next day, completely intact but in a different location. This is what happens to MP Kitchen one day. Its departure is so sudden, so final, that I can almost believe I've imagined the whole thing, but for the fact of the shanty's ghostly outline in the dirt. I continue down the road, perplexed. I am even more confused the following day when Nthabeleng's son, Neo, and I are returning from playing soccer. There it is—MP Kitchen, exactly as before—just on the opposite side of the Chinese trading post, like it fell through a rip in the cosmic fabric and re-emerged with the wrong coordinates.

Just as we notice the resurrected restaurant, the skies open and begin to soak us. Neo and I run for the shanty's doorway and duck inside. Everything is identical: 'M'e MP is stirring a giant pot of mutton, the single communal table is occupied with local VIPs having lunch, and every inch of the tiny shack is cramped with cooking supplies, burners, hot plates, and seasonings. MP looks up from her cauldron, understands we have come to take shelter from the monsoon, nods at us, and returns to her culinary tasks. The rain roars against the shanty's metal roof like the end times have come.

Papa: The *sine qua non* of the Basotho meal. Nothing is more important to the Mosotho stomach than *papa*, which is ground maize meal cooked in water, resulting in a dense, starchy mound that looks like a stiffer version of mashed potatoes. For shepherds, it may be the only food consumed during a meal. In more rural areas, *papa* is eaten with the hands and used to sop up any last scraps of *moroho*. At the Thia-La-La butchery, the steam trays are pillowed high with it. Out at the high school, students heft lunch plates laden with gargantuan domes of *papa*, along with beans or peas or *moroho*—and, on Fridays, the additional treat of pilchards (see below).

While I have grown fond of this corn mush, the thing I love best about *papa* is the utensil that accompanies it: the stick. Every kitchen, every smoky hut, every household in Lesotho has a wooden stick—a *lesokoana*—which is used for stirring and distributing *papa* from the common pot. In the villages, this stick is whittled down from a branch until about a foot long, perhaps a half inch in diameter. A certain amount of symbolism and ritual revolve around the *lesokoana*, including a rain-making game played between villages, where a young girl steals the *lesokoana* from the chief's hut and relays it, girl to girl to girl, until she is either caught or reaches her home village safely.

It is the elegance of this utensil that appeals to me, though. The *lesokoana* has no moving parts; there is nothing to rust or stain, nothing to clean or disassemble; it is immune from foodie obsessions over brand name or composition or provenance.

It is just a stick.

Pilchards: Canned fish spines in red sauce.

Steam Bread: The traditional Basotho bread; the dough is cooked over a pot of boiling water—instead of within an oven—for the fairly straightforward reason that Basotho huts don't have ovens. This cooking method produces a dense, moist bread with an oddly gummy exterior—an anti-crust—delicious nonetheless.

Stoney: This is ginger beer, which means it tastes like ginger ale plus methamphetamines. It is an unassuming milky white color and can be found in various locations across the African continent. In addition to being a good mixer for whiskey, Stoney is renowned for its curative powers. This according to Ellen, who chugged a bottle at the top of Moteng Pass after she barfed from altitude sickness.

Stout: Specifically Castle Milk Stout, which is a brand of beer that tastes a bit like Guinness and has a similarly dark body, although its nutty brown head distinguishes it from the classic Guinness "priest collar." It is Castle Milk Stout I am imbibing one night as I talk with the bartender Ntate Mokati, a friendly guy I run into frequently around Mokhotlong. I tell him I'm about to set out for the other side of town to meet some friends, and—as he is just finishing his shift—he says he will accompany me. I buy another quart of Milk Stout to share as we travel.

The darkness outside is complete. Cloud cover blots out the stars and the moon has not yet risen. It is only eight but it feels like the midnight of some prior century, my eyes refusing to adjust to the total black. I stay close by Mokati's side, keeping pace with the genial tone of his voice as he muses about reggae music and girlfriends and whether or not he believes in God. The night's depth is beyond comprehension. As we walk, Mokati occasionally sends a friendly greeting out into the void and a disembodied voice responds, sometimes just feet away. Then a shadowy outline takes human form and Mokati stops to chat for a moment. It is not clear to me whether Mokati knows these ghosts or not.

We drift through the abyssal dark like this for forty minutes, passing the Milk Stout back and forth as we talk. Briefly I wonder if we have passed into the afterlife—it is certainly peaceful enough, and I feel devoid of worry at Mokati's side. But eventually my destination emerges from the gloom and we stop to part ways.

Later, Mokati will appear in various unexpected settings around the country and greet me as if there is nothing odd about it. When Ellen and I attend a wedding in a distant village, there is Mokati, cracking jokes to a crowd of partygoers. Another time he emerges onto the *pitso* ground in the town of Mapholaneng during the King's forty-sixth birthday celebration. He high-steps his way onto the field at the head of a team of silver-suited dancers, lip-syncing along with music blasting from the PA, whirling and stomping before the tent where members of Parliament are seated. By this point Mokati's surprise appearances will no longer be surprising to me—not in Lesotho, this country of wormholes, of ripples and tunnels in the fabric of the land.

We stand in the sightless Mokhotlong night and shake hands; the warmth of his grip once again endows me with corporeal form. I give him the remaining Milk Stout since he has farther still to go, and then Mokati fades off into the night.

I stand for a while outside my destination, the massive weight of the stillness embracing me. I consider whether Ellen might be back from her business out of town. I want to tell her what I saw tonight, or didn't see. I decide it might be nice to simply wander back the way I have come, even without my Virgil, and so I do that, slowly. The ghosts are all about tonight, spirits moving close beside me, greeting me invisibly as we pass.

GOOD & BAD JOALA

This is a story about *joala*, or at least I think it is.

I should start by explaining *joala*. I know you don't know what it is, because I barely know what it is and I've had buckets of the stuff. *Joala* is Basotho-style corn-beer, or corn-liquor, or corn-something. And to be precise, it's actually maize-beer, not corn-beer, although it is occasionally sorghum-beer.

Generally speaking, you can identify *joala* by one of the following: either you are A) standing in the *joala* district of Mokhotlong, which is a row of shanties where grandmothers stir steaming industrial drums of possibly toxic byproduct, or you are B) down by the turn in the river, where the road curls up toward the hospital, and you are heading toward that slim crooked tree where the grandmothers now sit with their *joala* for sale, decanted into plastic buckets.

Generally speaking, though, you cannot speak generally about *joala*. Each *joala* is unique, each its own intoxicating snowflake. I've had *joala* that was the pale color of dead skin and I've had *joala* that looked like orange juice. I've sipped it from old coffee cans, sipped it from cereal bowls, sipped it from a jug being passed around the village hearth. There is no consistent *joala* experience.

The best *joala* I ever had was the brew 'M'e Malereko cooked up in a rinsed-out laundry detergent bucket. That batch sat behind a couch for two weeks, keeping its own counsel in the dark. When Malereko finally unveiled it at Nthabeleng's birthday party, it had mellowed into a lovely apricot color, sweet and winy on the tongue. At the birthday party, as I watched Nthabeleng and her siblings do a synchronized hop-step routine to pulsing clubby *kwaito* music, I dipped my cup into the communal barrel and watched as raisins bobbed to the surface. They looked like tiny dried mermaids coming up to wave hello.

ᎧᎥᎧ

Eventually, though, talking about *joala* is always talking about Retselisitsoe Mohlomi, he of oversized noggin and joyous drooling grin.

Retselisitsoe is one of the forty-some children who pass through the safe home during a typical year. Some children stay here for weeks or months, some even longer, until they can be safely reunited with extended family. Most of them are here because they have lost at least one of their parents. All of them are here because AIDS has rearranged the accepted tenets of how their childhood should work.

Retselisitsoe Mohlomi (like so many before him) arrives at the safe home a pre-corpse. He is HIV positive, a hollow-eyed skeleton with an oxygen mask engulfing his face. He lingers around the edges of death just long enough to ruin everyone's month.

And then he recovers. (See, this is what Nthabeleng does—takes really-should-be-dead babies and converts them into most-certainly-alive babies.) Gradually, gradually, Retselisitsoe's body adjusts to antiretroviral meds. His metabolism stabilizes. He acquires muscle mass and bone density. Later he learns to walk, which is what many children his age would have done a year prior. When I comment on this transformation, Nthabeleng yells at me, as she will do.

"Hey, *uena!* Don't you know yet—this place is where we turn babies into balloons!" She draws out the double-O sound in the word *balloons*, inflating those vowels in the same way that she inflates the children.

The better part of a year passes. Now Retselisitsoe is a fat and yowling toddler-tank. He is a doe-eyed bruiser, a knocker-down of children, a goofy stumbling future rugby star. The mental image of his initial form—that skeletal pre-corpse—is crumpled up and pitched into the wastebasket of unpleasant memories.

And finally, after a year, Retselisitsoe is healthy enough to return to his grandparents, who are caring for his four siblings in a small village about an hour's drive from Mokhotlong.

Do I need to say that both of his parents are dead?

☈.⌥.☈

Perhaps this sounds like a difficult life: five young siblings being raised by two decrepit elders. Assuredly it is. And in Lesotho, especially up here in the mountains, it is a far-too-common way of life.

But I must note, to be accurate, that Retselisitsoe and his siblings do have something special going for them—that maybe their situation isn't the absolute worst. This is because Retselisitsoe's grandparents are among the most endearing and resilient human beings I have ever encountered. But before I explain what is most striking about Retselisitsoe's grandparents, a bit of context on male-female interactions. In these outer reaches of Mokhotlong District, it is still culturally accepted, although now technically illegal, for a man to perform *chobeliso*: the kidnapping of a girl from her bed in dark of night to claim her as a wife. I have heard this practice—with the most disturbing of euphemisms— referred to as "proposing." Walking through town, I once saw a married couple pass within feet of each other and not make eye contact. Another time, as I walked into a party with a Mosotho friend, the mountain wind whipping around us, I realized that he was intending to leave his wife sitting there in the passenger seat of the car, where she would patiently await our return from the celebration. And while I am certain that many Basotho would raise eyebrows at some of our own dissolute Western behaviors, the simple fact is that gender interactions here often strike my outsider eyes as bizarre.

What is shocking then—against this backdrop—is that Ma and Pa Mohlomi, these two crusty souls eking toward their eighties, seem deeply happy to be married. Proud, perhaps, of their shared decades scraping together a living in an earthen hut on the side of a mountain.

And perhaps that raises a question. When two people do share decades in an earthen hut on the side of a mountain, how exactly do they scrape together a living, especially when that side of a mountain is in eastern Lesotho, notoriously devoid of arable land?

That answer, like all worthy answers, lies at the bottom of a bucket of *joala*.

ॐ

We have inched the 4WD along the edge of a gorge where down below small goats are capering over loose rock. Ellen and I are heading for the rondavel of Ma and Pa Mohlomi. We have come for *joala*.

This is how Ma and Pa Mohlomi make their living, brewing *joala* in large stinking barrels in their hut. As we approach, they are standing in the doorway like a Basotho version of *American Gothic*, ramrod straight and stone-faced. Then Pa Mohlomi puts his arm around Ma's shoulders and says *mosali oaka*, my wife. His nose accordions up as he smiles; she laughs like a teenager. Beside their rondavel an enormous hog is snuffling through the dirt, shaggy and mottled black and white, and on a nearby tree branch a scrap of white cloth flutters in the breeze, indicating homebrew for sale inside.

I should admit that our visit does not revolve entirely around *joala*. We have come mostly because we miss Retselisitsoe, that little piss-and-vinegar destructoid, and somewhat because we need a *joala* fix, but also because we are bearing a stopgap supply of his antiretroviral meds.

Ma and Pa Mohlomi, in addition to keeping Retselisitsoe happy, healthy, coddled, and clean, have also mastered his HIV regimen—a dizzying daily concoction of Medicine X (4 mL, morning and night) and Suspension Y (2 mL in the morning, 3 mL at night) and Syrup Z (3 mL in the morning, 2 mL at night)—despite the fact neither can read and neither has received even the most rudimentary medical education. But today they have gotten word to Nthabeleng that Retselisitsoe's med supply will run out before their next chance to get to the rural clinic, a several-hour hike beyond their village.

Inside, Retselisitsoe has just woken from a nap. He is disoriented and, perhaps understandably, begins screaming when he sees us. Ma Mohlomi slings him onto her back and wraps him in a blanket, assuring him that we are not on a repo mission for the safe home. Soon, in the comfort of Ma Mohlomi's swaddling, Retselisitsoe begins laughing and making faces at us. We swoon. Something about his enormous inverted pyramid of a head, something about his brute and oblivious pinball trajectory through the other children as he chased a rolling ball, something about his skeleton-to-calzone transformation, like a perverse before-and-after photo—it all inspires the crushing desire to wrap him in your arms and squeeze him into dough.

Once, when he was back at the safe home, I held him as I pulled a booger from his nose. It came out like a great green garden slug, occupying his whole nasal passage. Retselisitsoe's eyes went wide with the attendant release of pressure. He gaped rapturously at me, and for the first time I understood that parental and godlike desire to protect and soothe and banish pain.

We hand over the antiretroviral meds and Ma Mohlomi offers us a seat, a cylindrical chunk of log. Their rondavel is a squat circular hut, the piled-stone walls insulated with a plaster of mud and dung, the same cohesive mixture that makes up the flooring. A shard of mirror hangs on the wall next to a picture of Jesus, which is wrapped in protective plastic and which could be titled *White Jesus Returns from the Salon, His Lustrous Mane in Rolling Gentle Curls.* Chickens scuttle and dart between suitcases and nested washbasins tucked beneath the ancient single bed.

Now that we have transferred the meds, it is time to sample *joala.* Ma Mohlomi—with her imperious eyes and mouth perpetually on the horizon of an outright smile—skips over to the giant barrel of *joala* stewing in the corner. Retselisitsoe indulges us as we pull him onto our laps. His chunky body has regained that deep country scent, an intoxicating perfume of soil, rain, hay, sweat, minerals, and cookfire smoke. I nuzzle my face into the tight, tiny coils of his hair; he smells like a rutabaga freshly plucked from the earth.

We show Ma Mohlomi the bucket we have brought with us: a small cornflower-blue pail that a child might take to the beach, able to hold a half gallon of seawater or a half gallon of Basotho moonshine. *Joala* is always BYO container.

"*Ke bo kae?*" we ask, holding up the pail.

Ma Mohlomi eyeballs the bucket for a moment. "Two," she says.

As in two *maloti*. As in 0.20 USD. As in four nickels.

Ellen and I quickly huddle, agreeing that two *maloti* is ludicrous. Instead, we offer to pay twenty *maloti*, claiming we have no change and feeling okay with a self-imposed 900 percent markup. Ma Mohlomi smiles and Pa Mohlomi takes the bucket from us, dips it into the murky vat, fills it to the brim, and puts the lid back on. Then he scoops up an extra cup's worth for us to taste.

We sip the *joala* carefully and smile with delight. "It is excellent," we say.

It is not excellent.

I have come to realize that the batch Malereko cooked up—the sweet, winy raisin brew—was the exception, perhaps wasn't even *joala* at all. Real village *joala* is uniformly terrible. Take, for instance, this batch: it is a sour, porridge-like aberration. It has the tang of turned dairy, a cream-of-leek viscosity, and the scent of old carpet. Small mysterious chunks bob in and out of sight. Scraps of maize husk float by on their way to hell. This *joala* is warm—not room temperature, but actually warm—something that hints at the exothermic reactions taking place down in its brackish depths. The aftertaste is distinctly that of cured meats—perhaps a fine Genoa salami—salty and fatty and clinging to the tongue.

We drink it down and sigh contentedly. We have never tasted anything so sublime.

Now—too soon, too soon—it is time to go. We collect our *joala* pail and chat a few extra minutes in our hybrid Engli-Sotho. We take turns hugging Retselisitsoe and smothering him with kisses. We head out the door, past the crowd of curious milling neighbors, past the tree branch with the scrap of white cloth, past the gorge and the scrabbling mountain goats, and then head home. And only once, on the road back, does the *joala* bucket nearly explode, the plastic lid bulging, suddenly domelike—pulsing and expanding from the unknowable reactions taking place inside.

ᔐᔐᔐ

Now we have reached the end of this story about *joala*.

I suppose I hoped we wouldn't get here—hoped maybe we'd get sidetracked or wander down the trails of some other story. I thought maybe I could talk around the point for long enough, or tell this story like it really was just about *joala*, even though it really wasn't.

Some time has passed since our visit. Over a long holiday weekend—we will learn these details later—Retselisitsoe begins having diarrhea. He is sick, but not terribly so. Ma and Pa Mohlomi decide that they will take him into the rural clinic as soon as it reopens after the holiday.

Ma Mohlomi sets out on foot early Monday morning, trekking several hours through the mountains with Retselisitsoe swaddled to her back. When she arrives, she unwraps the blanket and passes Retselisitsoe gently to the nurses. Surely the nurses can see that he is already dead. Ma Mohlomi must understand this as well.

Only a few days have passed since he became sick. He never even seemed very ill, she tells us later—he is just suddenly gone, his quiet little body asleep.

Ma and Pa Mohlomi send word to the extended family of Retselisitsoe's dead father, the relatives who—according to Basotho kinship rules—have rights to the child's body, this child they haven't attempted to care for or know in any way.

Retselisitsoe's body lies wrapped in Ma and Pa Mohlomi's rondavel. A day passes before members of the dead father's family arrive to reclaim him. They take him and bury him without a funeral in another village.

Pa Mohlomi travels by donkey to see the child buried, then returns, upset that they haven't marked the grave or even used a coffin.

"Just a wooden box," he says. "If they didn't want to bury him, we would bury him."

This is how the other family sends Retselisitsoe into the earth.

꙳⸵꙳

It has been a month now since Retselisitsoe's death. Ellen continues to visit Ma and Pa Mohlomi, even though the NGO's business with them has technically concluded. Ellen tells them stories about Retselisitsoe's time at the safe home, about how much everyone loved him. When she heads out their way on her motorcycle, Ma and Pa Mohlomi grow happy; they can hear her coming through the gorge, the motorcycle announcing her presence with its onomatopoetic Sesotho name: *se-tu-tu-tu*.

Today Ellen has gone to their village to help with the harvest—autumn has arrived and the world has turned hay-colored, everything saturated in yellows and browns. She and the Mohlomis spend the day hacking through maize stalks with handheld sickles. Later Ma Mohlomi will gather the cobs and de-kernel them, run the piles of golden pellets through a hand-cranked mill to make maize meal.

Ellen has brought a small lunch for them, and at midday they sit and share food in the field. As she talks, Ma Mohlomi is fiddling with the glow-in-the-dark rosary she wears around her neck. She has a little ritual now, she says, that makes it easier to start her day. When she wakes up, before first light has crept into the room, she begins to mimic Retselisitsoe's tiny voice, calling out for his sister to set the kettle boiling—*It is late, It is late, Go out!*—just like he used to do each morning. Even in death he commands them, even in death he bends them to his indomitable toddler will.

But Pa is still angry, his milky eyes clouded, upset at the other side of the family. "No one was caring for them there," he says. "This is why we took in Retselisitsoe and his siblings. That other family didn't come to visit, they didn't know what was happening, they never helped us. Even when Retselisitsoe was at the safe home, they didn't care."

A silence settles over the group. Over the years, Ma and Pa have watched both of their own children die, and now one of their grandchildren.

"God is sometimes doing it like that," Pa says after a moment. "We have one ax to cut all the leaves—but sometimes it can cut through just the small ones and leave the strong ones behind."

Before she gets back on her motorcycle, Ellen gives them some pictures she has printed out, photos that hang now on the earthen walls of the Mohlomi rondavel: Retselisitsoe playing in the nursery, and running around the safe home grounds, and eating dinner with the other children, his face smeared with puréed vegetables. To me the pictures all look the same. Whether Retselisitsoe is laughing or crying, candid or posed, I can't help but see the sadness in his gaze, the mournful foreknowledge of his death.

꙰

Here's a memory I have of him.

Retselisitsoe—his name means *We give condolences*—is throwing a tantrum, screaming hysterically about something, probably nothing at all. He is wearing a pink and purple shirt that someone has donated, the words *Little Princess* stamped in rhinestones across the front. I take him in my arms and leave the nursery. We walk the hallways until he is calm.

We walk into Nthabeleng's empty office. I stand up on a chair, still holding him, so we can look out the high windows.

Suddenly Retselisitsoe is entranced, staring out at the land around him, captivated by the pickup trucks on the road, the meandering cattle, the children playing down by the river, the innumerable darting birds. He looks back at me, eyes wide: *Are you seeing this?* He stares up at the sky, pupils dilating. Then he looks back into the room, notices the ceiling just inches from his head, and reaches a cautious hand up to touch it. His gaze keeps shifting from the dimensionless blue span of the sky to the firm yellow plaster of the ceiling.

He looks at me in wonderment, trying to parse these two concepts, how funny it is, how strange, that there is ceiling above us, just over our heads, where there should be sky.

III.
AUTUMN
GROWING UP

During morning assembly, I hid in a pocket of shade under the eaves of a classroom building. The students were gathered in ranks facing the assembly leaders. I stood behind them, one thousand students in maroon and white, one thousand shaved heads, boys and girls alike, as the school required. They sung a ghostly fragile song, teenage voices rising in morning stillness, male and female tones, weight and counterweight. On certain beats they stomped their feet and puffs of dust rose around their ankles.

After class, I graded homework and watched some boys through the window as they did school chores. They were bent over, cutting weeds with dull hand sickles, pulling the grass up tall and sawing through. It reminded me of a poem from the Harlem Renaissance that I had taught as a student teacher: "Black reapers with the sound of steel on stones / Are sharpening scythes. I see them place the hones / In their hip-pockets as a thing that's done, / And start their silent swinging, one by one." I had asked the class what the poem was about. One kid said: Racism? Another said: Slavery? "Look at the language," I told them. "What mood is Toomer trying to foster here?" Isaiah spoke up then, a thin, sweet boy, and said, "It's about violence coming for you." Before the end of the year he dropped out of school, went to jail on a gun charge a month later. I don't think he was eighteen.

Sometimes I looked out at the students in my classroom and wondered what it meant to grow up in Lesotho. I knew that—statistically speaking— more than a quarter of my students had lost one or both of their parents. But the numbers don't always tell the story.

Outside the boys slashed at weeds. Pull taut, slit. I heard a shriek and ran to the window.

By the harvested plots of moroho, some girls were playing a riotous game, screaming happily as they tried to build a tower of small flat stones, racing to balance one atop the other before another girl could topple this precarious construction. They ran wild, drunk on joy, kicking up dirt and falling over themselves in laughter.

ON THE OCCASION OF BUYING SOMETHING FOR WHICH I HAVE NO NEED

Sunlight filters through the burlap shade and into our rondavel, which sits out back on the safe home property. It is early still—maybe six o'clock—but most of Mokhotlong has already kicked back its covers, up at dawn, asleep at dark, attending to the rhythms of a pre-electrified world. I have been pulled from my dreams by a clamor of bells. Shepherds hike past our rondavel daily, driving sheep into the mountains, the herd, hundreds deep, marching by like a parade of steel drummers: tiny clappers peal joyously against hand-welded metal bells that hang from woolly necks. The sobbing of the bells, Poe called it, but I don't think he had it quite right.

The din of bleating and tintinnabulation swells and then subsides. Later today, as I walk through town, I will see the mountainside undulating strangely, as if I am looking through a shimmering wall of heat. Then I will realize that the uncanny shifting of the mountain's surface is the movement of this same flock, grazing high above, a ripple in the fabric of the earth.

But for now I am up and out of bed. I have a plan. Today is Ellen's thirtieth birthday.

※.♥.※

As I walk into town, a man tries to sell me a pig, or a future pig, as he has no animal with him at the moment.

"Yes, this one, *kannete*, it is so nice. I know you will like it."

I tell the man I am not currently in the market for a future pig. He looks disappointed, but I do not buy livestock sight unseen. I continue up the hill, then stop and call back to the man. I tell him there is something I'm trying to buy today, but I am not exactly sure where to get it. I explain my plan. Would he know where I can find one?

The man looks puzzled. "You are a shepherd?"

"No, I am trying to purchase it for someone."

"This person is a shepherd?"

"No, I am just trying to purchase it."

The man stares at me for a moment, then points me toward an area of town, past the *joala* district where they cook maize beer in massive barrels, over toward the vegetable warehouse where they usually don't have vegetables.

"It is difficult to explain," I tell him somewhat apologetically.

The man stands and watches me go.

≈.♥.≋

Up ahead I see a small knot of children playing in a muddy cow pasture—six-year-olds who have not known the cleansing touch of water in some time. They clamber about in blankets and gumboots, their woolen shepherds' hats flopping around like rooster combs. From afar, their general appearance is that of a whirling localized dust storm. I've been observing their manic exploits as I come up the path, rock-throwing games and intense miniature soccer matches played with a bundle of taped-together plastic bags. One boy is chasing a rolling hubcap, goading it with a stick, and others push elaborate handmade toy cars, constructed from old hangers, rolling the vehicles over rough terrain on rusted Coke-can wheels.

Just before I reach this cluster of tiny hooligans, I see them retrieve a plastic horn from a runoff ditch. The horn is a souvenir from some forgotten soccer contest, a noisemaker used by fans to fill arenas with racket: a *vuvuzela*, an elongated yellow plastic tube which widens into a gentle bell-shaped mouth. On the weekends, men bring these horns to the local bars where they watch soccer, the *vuvuzela* being of totemic significance, an essential accoutrement on par with the giant foam fingers (*We're #1!*) brandished at American sporting events or the opera glasses and top hats wielded by rowdy patrons at La Scala. When the soccer matches are finished, the inebriated supporters of the winning side spill into mountain alleyways, trumpeting their sonorous joy into the Mokhotlong evening, prehistoric animal cries that echo off surrounding peaks as dusk deepens.

This is what the children have dredged from the muck at the precise moment I pass alongside them: a *vuvuzela*. I can see them pondering the horn's potential—can see the cartoonish cranking of their mental gears—just as they notice me. Their immediate and inchoate collective instinct is to run over to me, cheering and yelling *Nka! Nka!*—Take it! Take it!

I stand before them, eyeing it with apprehension, then glance back at the midden heap where the *vuvuzela* has been entombed for an unspecified period of geological time. The moment is pregnant with meaning, the children in a circle around me, waiting.

Wordlessly I take the horn and they trill with glee, shaking one another by the shoulders. I cannot understand how we have come to this point so quickly. I place the soiled instrument to my lips, an act that feels unspeakably intimate, trying to make as little physical contact as possible. I take a cautious breath, then blow. A weak moan emerges from the horn: a bleat, a flatus.

The children begin to laugh at me. The ringleader of these six-year-olds—the one who has thrust the weight of this responsibility upon me—takes the horn from me with a chastising air, as one might snatch car keys from a drunk. He says something to the rest of his cackling gang, but all I can catch is the word *ngoana*, which means *baby*. Then the ringleader places the *vuvuzela* against his lips and blows. The sound that issues forth is clarion, resonant, virile. Nearby cows look up. The children continue laughing.

I consider my options. It would be easy enough to continue down the road, no time for mission drift. I have nothing to prove after all: I am an adult and these are small children.

But I am also a man.

I grab the *vuvuzela* back from the ringleader. I brace myself, stance wide, fill my lungs, and blow—my embouchure perfect, my lips in deep spiritual union with the horn, vibrating at the frequency of celestial transmission.

Just as Athena sprang fully formed from the forehead of Zeus, so too does a sonic thunderclap leap from my trumpet. One of the six-year-olds falls to the ground. The tone is biblical and apocalyptic, the kind of fulmination that razes walled cities or unmoors glaciers. I drop the horn to the ground and saunter down the road.

Behind me, there is rejoicing.

⋊.♥.⋉

Farther along, I run into some teachers I know. Ntate Katleho, one of my Scrabble combatants, reminds me about his upcoming wedding. 'M'e Poho is coming back from the jail tucked down by the river, where she leads a prayer session. Both teachers give me looks of polite confusion when I tell them what I am looking for.

More children run after me on the road, calling for sweets or money: "Give me *lipompong!* Give me *chelete!*" I turn suddenly and yell, "*Ha kena lipompong!*" and the kids skid to a stop on their heels, fall on their butts laughing.

Now I see our friend Ntate Khatsa, a driver for the outreach team, who once gave me some insight into how the Basotho view my relationship with Ellen. Any traditional Basotho marriage involves a woman who is younger than her husband—even if just by a few days—although the preferred age gap is closer to three or four years. When I told Khatsa that Ellen was a year older than me—we were in the midst of a multi-hour drive with the outreach team—he fell into a deep silence. When he spoke again, he seemed uncomfortable, as if I had just informed him that I was married to my sister.

"Ah," Khatsa said, "ah no." He was fumbling for the right phrasing, venturing out and then retreating from his word choice, trying his best to bridge this impossible chasm. After some time, he said in a measured tone: "For Basotho people, that would not be ideal."

Even stranger is our childlessness. Producing offspring is an essential marker of adulthood in Lesotho, so to many people Ellen and I come across as some kind of benignly confused adult babies. When Ellen talks with grandmothers out in the villages, they don't ask *if,* they ask *how many*. She once told an old *nkhono* that she planned to finish her research before having children, and the woman began laughing sweetly. "Oh, *ngoaneso!*" she said—"Oh, my sweetheart!"—and patted Ellen's knee kindly, a gesture of support for a poor simpleton.

I wave to Khatsa from across the road, then pass our drunk neighbor, who staggers by and stops momentarily to steady himself against a piece of chain-link fence. He sees me and his eyes go wide. "NAY-*BAH!*" he yells. I have never seen the man sober, only in various shades of intoxication. I am unsure if his current bender extends from last night or has just begun anew, or whether distinctions like these can even be drawn. He works for the local government, a notary of some kind; birth certificates, passports, and subpoenas all must bear his stamp before they can become legal documents.

Here is Ntate Bokang, further down the road, the night watchman from the safe home. He is sitting on a tarp with his wife selling bananas, his daytime gig. Last week it was cabbage, before that apples, whatever is in surplus at the moment. I buy a banana and Bokang comps me a second one, cheerfully insistent that I take it, but then his face becomes serious.

"You have seen the very drunk one?"

"Yes, I greeted him just now."

"*Ache*, that man! I have been telling 'M'e Nthabeleng that the night guards must have a weapon. You must tell her. That man, the very drunk one, he was beaten so badly one night. Some men were waiting for him as he came home and they beat him! I shouted but I did not have a weapon to stop them."

For some time now, Bokang has been attempting to convince Nthabeleng that the organization should furnish the night watchmen with firearms, and recently he has enlisted me to prevail upon Nthabeleng's better judgment. It strikes me as doubtful that anyone is planning an armed incursion against a safe home filled with slumbering AIDS orphans, but I have hesitated so far in saying this directly to Bokang. I try to picture him, with his sweet smile and credulous eyes, gunning down these men who were drunkenly fighting in the road. I see myself returning to the grounds of the safe home late some sightless Mokhotlong night, rattling the gate as I unlock it, and Bokang emptying a revolver into me. I try to envision the other guard, the ancient Ntate Motsi, wielding a pistol—Motsi who can barely walk.

"I will suggest your idea to 'M'e Nthabeleng. But I think she will say no."

Bokang seems satisfied with this. Before I continue along, I tell him what I'm trying to purchase. He stares at me, a smile growing on his lips, and then he begins laughing.

"You are not a shepherd!" he calls out.

Bokang's wife is laughing too. This is the best joke I have ever told.

२.७.९

I have almost reached the place where I will buy Ellen's birthday present. My path through town has been rambling and unhurried.

I pass the permanently burned-down bar, just rubble inside, with men working every day to rebuild it and nothing ever progressing.

I pass a man with an enormous bull's head in a wheelbarrow. The head looks shockingly large when removed from its natural context; it fills the entire wheelbarrow. Its round, glassy eyes gaze into the recent past.

I pass the coffin shop. The PA system outside this metal shanty is blasting an old hip-hop song at deafening volume. I stop and listen to the line *It's getting hot in here, so take off all your clothes* as the man out front kneels in the dust and hammers together the sides of a casket.

Ahead, I can see sparks and the men welding.

२.७.९

The welders have a table and workbench set up along the road, out in the open air. Their tools are strewn about, but their metalwork creations are exhibited in orderly rows on the ground: small shelving units, footstools, and bells—a broad spectrum of handmade shepherd's bells, some as small as a deck of cards, intended for sheep and goats, and some as large as a loaf of bread, ponderous things that will hang from the necks of cattle.

Here at the welders' station, I will find a cowbell, which I intend to purchase for my wife, to honor her three decades of planetary existence. This is something she will find amusing, I think.

I run my gaze over the panoply of bells. Each is beautiful in a rough and unfinished way. They are crafted from scraps of metal, molded into hexagonal tubes and fused along the seams. Their edges are jagged and the sides of the bells are a deep steel blue, daubed with sienna and white whorls of rust. There are tiny nubs and metallic bubbles frozen in the surface. The clapper is an inch-long segment of rebar.

I tell one of the welders that I want to purchase a bell. He turns off his brazing torch and pulls up his goggles.

"You are a shepherd?"

I start to explain and then trail off. I shake my head. I am not a shepherd.

The welder shrugs, then lays his torch on the workbench and comes around front. We look at the bells together and he encourages me to ring them and listen to the differences in sound. I give one a shake. It is tremendous—a round, massive tone leaps from the mouth of the bell. I reach for another to test it, but the welder stops me. He is not pleased with this one, doesn't like its sound.

As I crouch to examine and ring various bells, a small crowd develops. Bystanders murmur, my behavior having moved into alien territory. No one can fathom why a non-shepherd would waste money on something so distinctly pastoral. But eventually there is acceptance, my actions filed away in the cabinet labeled *Weirdo Makhooa Stuff*.

Then people begin to advise me:

No, no, that one is too small.

Ah, but not that large. That is unnecessary.

That one is fine in size, but the tone, it could be nicer.

Finally I pick a mid-sized bell with—at least to my eyes—artful veining and subtle, strange discolorations. I give it a shake, then tell the welder that this is the one. People in the crowd nod. I have made a good pick. My wife will be well pleased, even if she can have no use for the bell, even if she is married to a non-shepherd dummy.

I think about trying to explain how this cowbell might sit proudly on our mantle someday, this otherworldly metal sculpture, but I am not sure how this will translate.

Once I read a short story called "Everyday Use," by Alice Walker, a story about a mother and her two daughters. The mother has a quilt, a family heirloom that dates all the way back to the days of slavery. She wants to pass this quilt along to her younger daughter, the quiet and practical homebody who still lives on the family farm. This enrages the older daughter, the cosmopolite, now off living in the city. She should have the quilt. She understands its aesthetic value and will treat it with honor. She will frame it and hang it on the wall of her apartment—the quilt is art! The younger daughter will ruin this quilt through everyday use.

I probably don't need to say that the older daughter is the villain in this story.

I pay the welder for his creation—the bell has set me back about thirteen dollars—and turn to the gathered crowd. They are awaiting closure, some final comment, since they are now invested in this purchase as well.

I do the only thing that feels right. I shake that bastard as hard as I can.

WHIPPING

On Thursday morning, I give a quiz to my Form A math students. Ninety-two erasers at the ends of ninety-two pencils trace ninety-two curlicues in the air. The classroom is humid and dense with teenagers, knobby, hormonal bodies suffusing the air with pheromones and desperate joy. The windows are fogged over—it is raining outside—but it is hot in the room and I am sweating through my clothes. I ask them if I can crack a window, allow the room to breathe.

"No, sir! The rain!"

The students hate the rain with unknowable fervor.

"Yes, but isn't anyone hot?" I ask as I move toward the windows. The students, it seems to me—in their burgundy wool uniform sweaters, their button-down dress shirts, their burgundy-and-gray-striped neckties—might appreciate some ventilation.

"Sir! The rain!"

I sigh and mop sweat from my person.

"Yes," I say, "the rain."

They watch me anxiously until assured I will not let the odious rain in. Ninety-two heads bow once again to their quizzes while the wind pushes at the wooden plank door, held shut by a small boulder.

The odors in the tiny room rise and fall in complex curious interplay: the gamey hum of ninety-two thoroughly unwashed teenage bodies, the musty reek of damp wool, the earthen scent of rain, and the oniony tang of my own thoroughly unwashed and non-teenage body. Permeating all of this is the aroma of campfire, which is the smell of rondavel living, a smell that clings to all bodies, all books, all clothing with astounding tenacity. It is the ember-laden memory of one thousand meals cooked inside over an open fire. Even when I am alone in the staff room grading homework, I can immediately tell which students live in rondavels further out in the mountains—as opposed to living here in town, where most people have stoves or hot plates—simply by the smoky aura wafting from their notebooks.

I patrol the classroom. The cinderblock walls are painted a timid cornflower blue. A schedule hangs in the back corner of the room, listing when the girls sweep out the room with brooms of dried grass, when the boys cut weeds outside with dull, rusty hand scythes. Now I come across a boy who has finished his quiz early. He has moved on to other homework, filling out a study sheet for his agriculture exam, stumped on a question that reads: *What are the four signs of a pig in heat?* He has written: 1) *the redding of the vulva,* 2) *the loss of appetite,* 3) *the mounting,* and 4) *??????* He taps his pencil on the paper as he stares out at the rain.

As I walk around the room, I try to picture how these children will emerge in adulthood. That boy is surely some echo of my old childhood friend Joe, a parallel-reality Joe, a kind and loyal boy who became a soldier and went off to war. That girl there is a rewound version of Nthabeleng, a future world-beater; she has that charge to her, the air around her ionized. And that girl in the third row is my sister Mary, it is undeniable, she has the same bashful grin, the same surprised laugh—I would hear that laugh after school as we tore through the tunnel on our bikes, suddenly pitched out of sunlight and into shocking darkness, before we surfaced sun-dazed on the other side of the train tracks, heading toward the mild chore of piano lessons. (Two years younger and she was already the more graceful and diligent musician; I had not yet mastered "Send in the Clowns," nor would I.) In different classrooms, I have come across incarnations of my wife, seen echoes of world leaders and celebrities, met variations on my parents—all of our personalities and idiosyncrasies shuffled and drawn from some common deck.

Now I come to Nkhopoleng—she of widest eye, of sweetest smile—who has also finished her quiz. She is chewing something as she sits staring through the chalkboard. But the students are not allowed to eat in class, so I ask Nkhopoleng what is in her mouth.

She stops mid-chew, slowly looks up at me.

She opens her mouth and sticks out her tongue, presenting an enormous half-masticated wad of notebook paper.

I try to formulate a response but nothing immediately comes to mind.

Suddenly I hear paper tearing behind me. I spin around and catch a second girl, now frozen, with a blank sheet of notebook paper halfway into her mouth.

"Why are you doing that?" I ask her.

Any student enrolled in the high school gets lunch every day—a gut-busting mound of thick, starchy *papa*, along with peas or beans or cabbage—so I know it is not hunger driving this strange behavior.

This second girl is on the verge of tears now. "Sir, I don't know," she says. Then she cautiously begins to chew.

I look back at Nkhopoleng, I look around the room. Everywhere students are silently chewing on mouthfuls of notebook paper, staring at me in wonder, ninety-two pairs of eyes trying to parse my unanswerable questions.

꒐.꒤.꒢

Later that afternoon, I come into the Math and Science staff room and find two boys lying on the ground. They look up as I enter, expectant and embarrassed. I pause, as I assume anyone might upon encountering such a sight: two high school boys lying on their stomachs in the faculty office, both in a state of high tension.

I am about to ask them what they are doing when my vallie, 'M'e Poho, calls me over. She asks me to check her work on a problem she is writing for an exam, and although I am still aware that these two boys are lying face down in the middle of the room, I briefly become engrossed in the question. I have not yet realized it is an attempt to distract me from the situation I've walked into.

Poho and I are sketching out solutions on the back of a curriculum guide—stamped, like all school-issued material, with the slogan *Fight AIDS, be faithful, and live!*—when Ntate Hlompho enters the room.

He looks directly at me and stops. A sheepish look crosses his face.

"Oh," he says, flatfooted.

Hlompho has tiny eyes that nuzzle slightly too close together, as if seeking each other's warmth. He is mild-mannered and generally inoffensive—a milksop of a man, the Cheerios of people—a person whom the female teachers often gently mock behind his back. Hlompho looks down at the two boys on the floor and then back at me. He gives a quiet chuckle and shakes his head. "Ntate Moshoeshoe," he says, "you will have to cover your eyes."

Pauses.

"I am about to skin an elephant."

It is at this moment that I register what he is holding in his hand: a three-foot length of thin rubber hose. At the same moment that my brain processes this information, Hlompho begins to whip the shit out of these two boys with the rubber hose. He whips them across their thighs and across their backsides. He lustily heaves his body into the whipping, his arms in full torsion, his torso snapping efficiently and then recoiling, everything about him elastic. It is an act of stunning brutality—and yet there is something obscenely graceful in the way his body moves, his body which is normally so artless. After the first few blows, as he alternates between the two boys, he begins yelling something in Sesotho.

The boys are rolling in pain, rocking from side to side, turning over onto their backs to beg restraint, eyes welled with tears. Then they roll again onto their stomachs because Hlompho will hear no petitions for clemency, looming ferociously over them, and he will whip them across their fronts if he has to.

Before I continue, a digression on the physics of whipping:

A whip, to reach its maximum potential for pain distribution, must find a delicate balance between Flexibility and Mass. Too much Flexibility and the whip becomes unmanageable, like a strand of wet spaghetti. Too little Flexibility—the stiffness of a garden hose, say—

and there is no real action in the whip, no *bite*. You have moved from whipping into beating. There is also Mass to consider: a whip that is too light produces no impact, too heavy and it can't generate the velocity needed for that skin-lacerating *crack*. The three-foot length of pliable rubber tubing that Hlompho currently wields is, not surprisingly, the optimization of the Flexibility-Mass graph, because Hlompho is a high school math teacher.

The two boys extend their arms beseechingly, but each time the whip is already accelerating downward and they roll again onto their stomachs. I can see the emotions cycling across their faces throughout the ordeal: first wide-eyed entreaty, then clenched agony, and finally—in those micro moments just after the whip bites, their faces pressed against the linoleum—knuckle-whitened loathing.

This whipping seems to stretch out indefinitely, although it probably only lasts a few minutes. The rawness of the moment—the sheer intimacy of what I am witnessing—has unmoored me. At a certain point, I become aware that other teachers are staring at the proceedings too. Their attitudes range anywhere from clear discomfort to yawning complacency.

Eventually, I leave the room and walk home. I walk in silence across the autumnal plateau, feeling violent and guilty.

ב.ט.ג

Friday is here and I can tell the students are bored. I am bored too. We are bored at each other. We have been working on fractions for several decades and we are making no headway. And it is Friday. Perhaps I mentioned that.

"We are going to play a game today," I explain to the ninety-two. They are packed into the narrow cinderblock room, sitting two and three to a bench. "I will write a fraction on the board. You will race to see who can put the fraction into its lowest terms. Do you understand?"

Yes, sir. They answer in chorus.

"I will call on whomever I see raising a hand first."

Yes, sir.

"Any questions?"

No, sir.

"So I will write the fraction on the board and—"

Lowest terms, sir.

I go to the board and begin to write, using my notebook to shield the fraction from their eyes. This strikes them as hilarious and they roar with laughter. I finish writing the fraction, then look back at them, still holding my notebook in place.

They burst from their seats, hands raised, snapping fingers at me, nearly toppling over to get my attention, trying to resist stampeding the board, begging to be called on, ninety-two baby bird voices calling out in desperate unison:

Sir! Sir! Sir! Sir! Sir! Sir! Sir! Sir! Sir! Sir! Sir! Sir! Sir! Sir! Sir! Sir! Sir! Sir! Sir! Sir! Sir! Sir! Sir! Sir! Sir! Sir! Sir! Sir! Sir! Sir! Sir! Sir! Sir! Sir! Sir! Sir! Sir! Sir! Sir! Sir! Sir! Sir! Sir! Sir! Sir! Sir! Sir! Sir! Sir! Sir! Sir! Sir! Sir! Sir! Sir! Sir! Sir! Sir! Sir! Sir! Sir! Sir! Sir! Sir! Sir! Sir! Sir! Sir! Sir! Sir! Sir! Sir! Sir! Sir! Sir! Sir! Sir! Sir! Sir! Sir! Sir! Sir! Sir! Sir! Sir! Sir! Sir! Sir! Sir! Sir! Sir! Sir!

It is madness.

So I yell "*Tholang, bo-abuti le bo-ausi!*" and they become quiet.

"You are raising your hands because you think you know the answer?"

Yes, sir.

"But you haven't seen the fraction yet."

No, sir.

"So how could you know the answer if you haven't seen the fraction yet?"

Yes, sir.

For a moment I almost lose my teacherly composure, I almost smile. "Okay, when I take my notebook away, you look at the fraction, and *then* you try to put it in lowest terms. Is everyone ready?"

Yes, sir.

I shift my notebook one millimeter, just to see what will happen. The fraction is still completely hidden from view.

They burst forth again, hands raised, fingers snapping, straining out of their seats, ninety-two central nervous systems in synaptic meltdown.

I can no longer resist temptation. I choose Nkhopoleng, sitting on the front bench, she of widest eye, of sweetest smile.

"Nkhopoleng, yes, what is the answer?"

The classroom falls into an intergalactic silence.

Nkhopoleng: just one second ago in a frenzy to be called on, frothing with anxiety that she might not be called on, now suddenly and horrifyingly called on. Terror radiates from her wide eyes as she attempts to process the enormity of her situation. I can see the gears in her brain—still a bright brassy gold, still well-oiled and rust-free—I can see her brain gears lock up behind those translucent eyes. Her body settles into glacial stillness, as if I might somehow look past her.

"Nkhopoleng, you have the answer?"

Silence. For years.

"Nkhopoleng, yes?"

Finally a tiny voice, tinier than the tiniest grain of sand: "Eight, sir?"

I stare at her. I am bordering on sadism by this point.

"Eight? You think the fraction, in lowest terms, that is still hidden behind this notebook, that you have not yet seen, is the number eight?"

"Yes, sir?"

I sigh and let the moment ride out. "Well, you're close. Anyone else?"

☙✺❧

I did, sometime later, ask what precipitated the whipping.

Hlompho had caught the two boys in the middle of an end-of-exams prank. They were carrying a dead rat with them, which they planned to leave in the school's kitchen with a lunch plate in front of it. The rat—the boys were hoping, in an attempt at pungent commentary—would appear to have consumed the daily meal and keeled over.

During my first week of teaching in Mokhotlong, one of my colleagues informed me that I too would be expected to punish when the children misbehaved.

Ntate Lebo, from the Scrabble cohort, is a young man only a few years graduated from this selfsame institution, fresh from teachers' college now. "What kind of punishment?" I ask him, thinking about 'M'e Khauhelo and her willow switch—prized for its thin, elegant form, its superior firmness, its tightness of recoil—which she slices down across the open palms of small girls who have violated the dress code. I think about Ntate Thabiso and the section of rubber hose that he keeps close at hand, a warning to students about how they will get hit if caught speaking Sesotho and not English on the school grounds.

Lebo sighs. He can't be any older than twenty-one, this boy teacher. Months later, I will run into him on the main road and he will excitedly tell me about the saxophone lessons he is taking at his church. He is thin and gentle and—yes, that is the only word. Lebo is the physical embodiment of gentleness.

"As for punishments," he tells me, "many of the teachers beat the students because it is easiest. But some teachers make the students do work instead, like cutting weeds or carrying rocks up from the river."

"What do they do with the rocks?"

"They make them carry the rocks back down to the river."

I ask him what type of punishment he prefers.

"Well, it is difficult. The punishment for the student must not also be a punishment for the teacher. But I do think the punishment should be something useful. For me, I make the students write poems, since I am an English teacher. They hate this writing too too much, because if the poem does not rhyme, they must write me a new one. But the best thing is that they are practicing and learning."

Lebo asks me what I'm going to do when the time comes.

I think for a moment, wondering about the ways in which violence radiates out into the world, transmitted neighbor to neighbor, teacher to student, amplifying and receding—these small personal moments of degradation.

"Poems," I say. "I'll have them write poems too."

᠅

Friday, late afternoon:

We leave the classroom, teacher and student alike pulsing with buoyant weekend joy. The end of the school year is on the horizon as well—we can all feel it coming. We are buzzy and humming with that mild electricity at the base of the spine.

We come out of our various classroom buildings and into the assembly space outside. Now here is the student body mobbed in front of the Form A building—the first year students' building—the whole school gathered and jeering, calling for Form A students to show themselves. My ninety-two are out in front of the building, milling about with their peers, awkward, smiling, unsure.

When I ask one of the teachers what is going on, he turns to me and says: "Oh, they are mocking them." He is surprised I don't know that today is the day the student body gathers to mock the first-year students.

Then he comments casually, "And now they will beat them."

This is how the rock fight begins.

A granite hail pours from the heavens, falling first upon Form A students, flung skyward by the gathered upperclassmen, and then, in retaliation, a return volley from Form A, the air alive with projectiles, chunk after chunk thudding: rock, pebble, stone, knot, brick, clod, clot. Children are running, screaming with hilarity and fear, looking for cover, looking for ammo.

Perhaps it is inevitable.

Nkhopoleng—she of widest eye and sweetest smile and so very very small—Nkhopoleng staggers away from Form A, swaying woozily, her wide eyes glazed now, her eyelids beginning to droop, her head streaming blood in bright red rivulets, a little delta across her forehead.

Nkhopoleng slumps over like wet snow coming off an angled roof.

It is then that the teachers begin yelling at everyone to stop the rock fight—*For shame!*—this rock fight they all knew would happen.

It is then that Hlompho runs in, scoops her up in his arms, picks her up like nothing, and heads for the hospital.

PORTRAIT OF A PATH
THROUGH TOWN

Ellen and I are making our way along the secret footpath, talking about nothing. We have wandered into a discussion about old sitcoms.

"*Cheers*?" I ask her. "The TV show *Cheers*? With Woody and those guys? It's one of the most beloved shows in television history."

"Yeah, I don't know," Ellen shrugs. "I just always found it too dark."

"What do you mean? That show was relentlessly goofy."

"No, you know: *dark*. It was always so dark down in that bar, no natural light. I just wanted those people to get some air, go run around outside or something."

We pause to step over some barbed wire on the hidden footpath.

"I think that's the most Canadian thing you've ever said to me."

≈.ɣ.≈

There is a hidden footpath that winds serpentine through the camptown, nosing between houses and curving across fields, disdaining perpendicularity as it meanders diagonal-ish through Mokhotlong. The path begins as a thin dirt strip out near the *pitso* ground—that flat stretch of land where town meetings take place—wide enough only for feet placed in single file. It quickly snakes between two stretches of homemade barbed-wire fence and then ducks out of sight. Experienced path-goers know to walk sideways here to keep the barbs from snagging hungrily in shirts or pants or dresses. On one side of this barbed-wire throughway, a small field of maize serves as a buffer from the road, and for a while path-goers are completely hidden, an odd and delightful sensation here in the middle of town. Soon the path emerges from the maize and comes upon planted rows of *moroho*—spinach, kale, chard—the boundaries of an old man's property. This grandfather, *ntate moholo*, is out in his backyard every day, digging, stacking, dragging, prying, chopping. He pauses and waves, looking scholarly with short dark hair and a silver goatee.

The path then empties onto a small cow pasture—home to four or five bovine sunbathers, their tails steadily tallying seconds—and continues past an unfinished house, perpetually under construction. Abandoned cinderblocks lie scattered around the cow pasture. Now the path jinks boldly down an alleyway and through someone's backyard. Another low barbed-wire fence must be hurdled—a challenge for dress-wearers and those wrapped in traditional blankets—and then a clothesline must be ducked underneath. Here the path disgorges onto the road lined with *joala* shanties, where old men sit out front drinking their homebrew and laughing at a joke they beat to death back in the early nineteenth century.

ৡৣৢ

Ellen and I are picking our way along the hidden path when we come to the mini pasture. Instead of sunbathing cows, though, we find several *mokhotlo* birds—the southern bald ibis, the town's namesake. In Sesotho, the letters -*ng* at the end of a word often indicate place, so the name "Mokhotlong" literally means "*mokhotlo* place." Or, in our own personal patois, "Bald-Ibis-Land." The *mokhotlo* is omnipresent here, familiar through its awkward hitch-step and squawking choke-cry. The bird's Latin name, *Geronticus calvus*, is apt—it means "bald old man." The curving orange beak comes attached to the face of an elderly butler.

"Have you ever noticed," Ellen says, "that a *mokhotlo* sounds exactly like a person trying to imitate a *mokhotlo*?"

Before I can finish rolling this piece of recursive logic through my head, she demonstrates, producing a throttled shout from the back of her throat. The birds, generally fearless, bolt for the heavens.

Now we pass *ntate moholo* digging in his garden. Soon we are hidden in the maize stalks, invisible, passing sideways through the barbed-wire fences.

"I went out looking for a man named Kapoko today," Ellen tells me. "Nthabeleng told me I should find him—a grandfather raising his two young grandsons by himself."

Ellen had set out for his village on her motorcycle and was met at the road by two grandmothers, laughing as they hobbled down the hill to greet her. "We saw you coming on your horse!" one called out. The women sent Ellen up the hill, where she found another old grandmother, an ancient and blind *nkhono*, who was very slowly working her way toward an outhouse, inching along, nearly motionless, holding onto a piece of wire that had been run between the outhouse and her rondavel. This was Ntate Kapoko's mother, and it was he who had run the guideline for her.

Ellen sat talking with *nkhono* in the cooking rondavel while they waited for Kapoko to return. The small space was immaculately ordered. Their set of enamel crockery was laid out on a bench along the wall with cups, plates, and bowls leaning against each other in precise repeating patterns, both to allow for efficient air drying and as visual embellishment, a decorative border—aesthetics emerging even in the simplest things. Mats sat folded beside the crockery, storage buckets nested in a tower, and the mud plaster floor was perfectly swept. There was not an extraneous thing in the rondavel, every inch optimized.

"Yes, he is taking very good care of his grandsons," *nkhono* told Ellen. "You can see. He is cooking, he wakes up early to fetch the water, he washes them." She spoke proudly. "*Kannete*—he is like a woman in the household!"

Soon Kapoko himself arrived, a thoughtful man in his sixties, with a certain intensity simmering beneath the surface of his words. One of his grandsons, Jesi, was hanging tightly to his pants leg. Kapoko's wife had left the family long ago, and he had raised their two children by himself. Then, several years ago, his grown daughter returned to the village, dying of AIDS-related complications. He nursed her in her final days, and after she was gone he took on the responsibility of her two boys.

He and Ellen were discussing his experience as the main caregiver for his grandsons—the challenges he faced raising the boys alone, the routines of daily life—when he echoed a comment that *nkhono* had made earlier.

"This boy, Jesi?" Kapoko said, rubbing his grandson's head, "he thinks of me as the mother. He doesn't know his mother, he only knows that his mother is me."

Jesi ran outside to play, aware he was the topic of conversation. He picked up a stick and began trying to swat the leaves off a tree, he and some other boys taking turns.

Kapoko continued: "Sometimes he can even say *Ntate Kapoko, are you my mother?* I tell him that his mother is Pulane, but he doesn't understand. *Where is she? Where has she gone? What will she bring me when she comes back?* But he is just four. He doesn't understand when people are saying his mother is dead. He only sees that I am the one giving him food, that I am the one sweeping and cleaning, doing laundry, doing everything—so he says I am his mother."

᎐᎗ᎊ

At the safe home, the house mothers stare in wonder whenever Ellen hops onto her motorcycle. They laugh in amazement when they see me sweeping our rondavel or doing the laundry. It is easier for us *makhooa* to buck culturally embedded gender roles, I think—the Basotho are willing to accept our irregularities as bizarre and probably harmless—but no one quite has an answer for Kapoko. If you ask any Basotho whom the best caregivers are, the answer is always *women*, fundamentally and unchangeably *women*. Yet Kapoko's skill and dedication in raising his children and grandchildren is indisputable, and so he and the few others like him remain a marvel out here in the mountains, referred to in female terms, unable to fit neatly within an established paradigm, incomprehensible as solely male even to himself.

This doesn't seem to bother him, though; Kapoko is not the type to genuflect before social norms. In the cooking rondavel, he told Ellen another story, about the time they came to take his grandsons away.

When Kapoko's daughter returned to the village a few years back, it was clear that she was dying. "Her stomach was swollen," he says, "and she refused to take the pills. She was ready to go home."

Nkhono is sitting next to him, listening. "She died in his hands," she says. "That girl died in his hands."

Jesi was very sick too, but Kapoko knew the matter was beyond his abilities, so he brought the boy into the hospital. Jesi stabilized there, gradually, and after a few weeks returned to Kapoko's household.

"*Kannete!*" interjects *nkhono*, "he is doing so well! Jesi is a man now. And always talking, talking—*jooooooeee!*—he was not like that before!"

Jesi has been listening outside the door and takes this moment to run back inside and flop dramatically over his grandfather's knee. He remains there, casually draped, trying to get a handle on what the grown-ups are talking about.

Kapoko is leaning forward now, his eyes lit up, an edge in his voice.

"But when Jesi was healthy, the other family came to take these boys. The father's relatives."

Kapoko is referring to the patrilineal nature of Basotho society. Traditionally—even legally—Jesi and his brother "belong" to the dead father's side of the family, no matter who has been caring for them, no matter who has raised them, the same situation that Ma and Pa Mohlomi found themselves in after Retselisitsoe died.

"Those relatives came to take the boys, do you hear? And I stopped them in the road."

Jesi is sitting on Kapoko's lap now.

"I told them that my daughter had come to me very sick. I told them her marriage was not good, they had not paid all the bridewealth. And after the husband was gone, she was not living well in their village—*kannete!*—they had not been caring for her there."

Jesi is tunneling deeper into his grandfather's arms.

"I was the one who cared for her when she was dying. And after she was dead, I contacted the other family, but they would not come to see her buried. All these things I did by myself."

He is holding Jesi tightly as he speaks, no longer addressing Ellen.

"And now you come after some months, when these boys are healthy, after I have been caring for them—and you say you are coming to take these children? And I say to you: the children of *whom*?"

Kapoko sits back after a moment, stirs from his memory. He looks down at Jesi, then looks back at Ellen.

"So they went away without anything. There was nothing they could do."

𝕽.𝕺.𝕾

As Ellen and I walk back up the hill toward our rondavel, I find myself thinking about my own grandfather, gone for some time now but a giant still in my mind. I can see him standing in the shade of sturdy oaks during a childhood baseball game, watching me from across the distance as I fidget in the outfield, praying the game won't encroach upon my peaceful territory. Even in the shadow of those oaks, he is towering. When my siblings and I were little, he often came to watch us, and I revered him, although reverence always incorporates some portion of fear.

Like most childhood fears, it was unwarranted, but it was especially strange to discover him so much smaller by the time I was in high school. By this point his health was diminished and I was coming to his house after school to help him shower and dress. In the bathroom, I would position him on a plastic shower chair and wash him; afterward, I would settle him on the edge of the bed, shroud him in a towel and rub his head dry, find socks to pull over tender gnarled feet. There in his bedroom we would talk secretly about nothing, the room washed in afternoon stillness.

Soon enough Jesi will learn a variation on these intimacies. Less than ten years separated my grandfather—looming invincible among the oaks—from that plastic shower chair. And I too will inherit my grandfather's seat eventually, will come to understand these intimacies from a different perspective, shared with someone whose name I do not yet know.

For now, though, I like to think about what came after the shower: dressed and slapped with aftershave, I would help my grandfather into a wheelchair and we would glide together through his house, moving in silence as we played an old Louis Armstrong record, skimming smoothly across the sunroom's parquet floor.

IN THE REALM OF
VANISHED BEASTS

Ellen and I have ventured down into the lowlands. We descend the Maloti mountain range in a 4WD, bypass meandering cattle, bisect clots of unruly goats, and eventually land in Maseru. We are in a bar there when we hear a tantalizing archeological rumor: dinosaur tracks, a man tells us, in the nearby town of Roma. The real deal, he says, the eons-old tracks of the Terrible Lizards, petrified proof that our little rock has taken a few spins through the solar system.

Only thirty minutes away, we think, *dinosaur tracks.* When else would we have the chance?

Here's a thought experiment. Let's say there really are dinosaur tracks within a heartbeat's drive of a nation's capital city. Now imagine that the nation is the United States and the city is Washington, DC. There are neon-green billboards along every highway within a five-hour drive, tourist packages for families on vacation, local celebrity endorsements, posters and coffee mugs and T-shirts that read "I Saw the Dino Trax & All I Got…"—a maze of stagnant lines and melting ice cream and teenage staff in candy-colored polos.

Back in Lesotho, the most concrete piece of information we could gather was that the dinosaur tracks were maybe somewhere on the western side of town.

ꘘ.ꗏ.ꕔ

The town of Roma is quiet. One could conceivably drive through Roma and not notice that one had done so. The sleepy main road runs past Lesotho's lone university and some deserted restaurants; other notable attractions along this route include an abandoned tennis court—weed-choked, cracked, netless—and a relatively new basketball court, where both hoops are swiveled away from the field of play like former lovers unable to bear eye contact. Gorgeous sandstone cliffs dominate one end of town, pale white rock that glows beneath patches of emerald scruff. The main road dips through a little canyon here and the sandstone turns luminescent in the late afternoon, the homebound sun breathing mysterious life into the cliffs. And then you are out of Roma again.

We drive aimlessly through town, searching for any sign of the dinosaur tracks, but there is not a billboard, poster, brochure. We ponder the single cryptic datum we have collected: something about the western side of town. But here we are at an impasse, as there is no western side of town. There is only a main road running generally north-south, with the university on the east side of the road and a tiny residential neighborhood on the west side—a neighborhood that almost immediately abuts onto a mountain. This neighborhood does not seem like a place to find dinosaur tracks. It seems more like a place that fell asleep on the couch watching *Jeopardy!*

Lacking other options, we proceed into the neighborhood, through narrow lanes of corrugated-metal shacks and two-room cinderblock houses. We are on an unpaved dirt track. Now we are possibly driving through a backyard. Finally—the first sign of life—we see a young girl behind her house playing with a dog. The dog is trying again and again to leap up and lick the girl's face, while she dodges away laughing. This girl is about thirteen, chubby, barefoot, and wearing a dirty white tank top. Her hair springs out from her scalp as if she has been mildly electrocuted. She has a peach-colored scar across her forehead and bright eyes.

"Do you know about the dinosaur footprints?" I call out to her in English, after greeting her in Sesotho. I wonder if she understands me and I briefly consider trying to pantomime a dinosaur, but this seems offensive to everyone involved.

The girl nods yes.

"Can you tell us how to get there?"

Now she comes up to the car. She starts speaking quickly, and in Sesotho, directing us with her hands, motioning left, then right, then right, then left, then up into the sky. She sees us struggling to keep up, then stops and says in English: "I will take you." Without further discussion, she hops into the backseat. I scan for some parental figure but the area is deserted, emptied out.

We briefly consider the ethics and safety of letting this girl join our half-baked sojourn, but I can so clearly remember from my own childhood that desperation for something, *anything*, to happen. My memories are of a boring (read: idyllic) Chicago youth, trying to animate our pacific neighborhood, prowling leafy back alleyways with my three siblings as we partook in light arson, exploding old aerosol cans to underwhelming result. We dreamed wild fantasies rambling through those secret precincts of childhood—what really *was* going on in that creepy wig shop, we would ask each other, cranking ourselves into a frenzy. No one had ever seen a soul enter or leave the place, a grungy single-story building whose entire façade was a wood-paneled blank, a level of secrecy that clearly marked it as a house of murder. (It had not occurred to us then that elderly gentlemen prefer privacy while trying on hairpieces.) Once, my younger sister Mary, in a feat of incredible courage, opened the door to the wig shop, peered into the gloom, and then fled. Inside she had seen an old man asleep on a ratty couch, wearing only his old man boxers and his old man undershirt, his skin shining pinkly through the worn cotton, more terrifying than anything we could have conjured.

It must present an impossibly enticing opportunity, then, to play host to strange *makhooa* visitors on a deathly still Sunday afternoon. The girl in our backseat is smiling and bobbing her head to some internal music, awaiting our decision. Ellen shrugs. Off we go.

Our tiny directrix steers us through the neighborhood, our path twisting and turning and doubling back on itself. There are no gridded neighborhoods in Lesotho, where everything must eventually bow to the contours of the earth. We curl through a residential labyrinth, then emerge, then slowly begin to ascend the smallish mountain that forms the immediate backdrop of the neighborhood.

Now we are climbing higher, the truck's engine churning. The housing here is no longer rectangular but circular, like the thatch-roofed rondavels we know in Mokhotlong. Our surroundings quickly turn deep country, with any lingering ninety-degree angles windblown into curves. A donkey roaming the mountainside brays at us. There is no longer anything resembling a road.

As we continue up the mountain, we begin to develop a small entourage. Children follow our truck, Pied Piper style, as we aim skyward. They have emerged from fields of maize, from behind boulders. We are moving so slowly across the terrain that this cadre of shoeless children can jog beside us, behind us, in front of us—we look like a miniaturized version of a presidential motorcade, the children ringing our truck like a complement of very cheerful Secret Service agents. Two boys are running beside my window, laughing and calling out *"Ke kopa lifti! Ke kopa lifti!"* and as I lean out to say "Sorry, no lift," Ellen slows to cross a gap in the non-road. One of the boys grabs hold of my hand, has now suddenly jumped onto the runner of the moving vehicle—"No," I'm telling him, "you've got to get down!"—and before I can do anything, before I can process what is happening, the boy has climbed in through the open window and plopped himself onto my lap. The second boy nimbly follows suit and suddenly I have two village boys, ages seven and nine, piled on top of me, laughing wildly at their boldness.

Ellen stops the truck. There is really no other option.

Now the floodgates open: the throng sends up a cheer and the remaining children clamber into the car. They are sitting on top of each other, stacked in a mad jumble of scrawny limbs. I do a quick head count. In addition to Ellen, myself, and our original guide, eleven more kids have packed into our truck—ranging between four and twelve years old—putting a total of fourteen passengers in the 4WD, a whole clown car's worth of child endangerment.

Watching all of this from the doorway of her rondavel is an old *nkhono*. She shakes her head, coughs out a rickety laugh, and waves us on. Ellen sets us into motion again and puts some *famo* on the radio, the accordion and bass rattling the speakers, and with this we have completed our transformation into a fully operational Basotho taxi. We continue along in a state of hilario-chaos, the kids stomping their feet and singing along to Phoka, belting the lyrics with atonal gusto, laughing and toasting the two boys who breached the siege wall.

We creep up the mountain, ten minutes farther, and then our guide tells us to stop.

"We are here," she says.

We pile out of the car, all fourteen of us. By now, even more children have seen our curious progress and have come to join us, upwards of thirty kids crowding around as our guide takes us on foot for the last stretch. The wind is whipping as we trek across a flat span of ancient rock.

"There," our guide says, and points to the ground.

I look. There is nothing.

I squint and look around, trying to be polite. "Where?" I ask.

"There," she says again, and points emphatically to a spot a few inches in front of me.

There are vague indentations in the rock, filled with rainwater. Shallow wells eroded into the stone by centuries of rain and wind.

I start laughing. If those are dinosaur tracks, then I've seen thousands of dinosaur tracks since I've been in Lesotho. They are depressions in the rock, they are nothing at all.

"And there," she says. "And there," pointing all around us.

I start examining some of the other pools of water. Ellen is hunched over too. And now that I look closely—

Well.

I stand up to get perspective, trying to take in these indentations. Each one has three angular toes, like the tines of a fork were pressed into the soft dough of the earth millennia ago. Suddenly I see one that I know is the real thing, feel an immediate clench in my gut. It is instantly recognizable, iconic, the tread of some long-dead proto-lizard, like an illustration torn from *The Encyclopedia for Precocious Children.*

≈.❖.≈

In the middle distance, the pale sandstone cliffs are pulsing as the sun slips toward the horizon. Ellen is doing cartwheels for the kids and I am taking pictures, trying to capture the impossible vista. We run our hands over the footprints of strange vanished beasts, reclaim them briefly from the realm of myth. There are no signs or velvet ropes up here on the outcropping; our experience has not been curated; we make of it what we want. As the light softens, I sit on the rock and press my hand into one of the tracks, trying to make it fit. It is hard not to consider one's place on the timeline.

Soon we'll head back down and return our guide to her sleepy neighborhood. We'll thank her for her expertise and press *maloti* into her hands, money she hasn't asked for, and she'll rub the peach scar on her forehead, pocket the coins, and run to her yard with tongue tucked happily between teeth. Her dog will bound toward her in eager greeting.

But we don't have to leave this place just yet. We can sit here a while longer, bathing in the cool air and studying dinosaur tracks. We can attempt to suss meaning, or not. The tides of entire species have come in and then washed to sea since these treads were trod, whole civilizations built up from the clay only to melt away in rain. I scan the village's worth of children clambering around the rocks with us. What have any of us learned about durability and its opposite during our transit?

But that lavish sunset is lighting the world on fire, so we scramble on undaunted, hoping to leave our incomprehensible tracks for whatever beasts come after. We'll leave them hypothesizing about our glorious unimaginable plumage, guessing all our colors wrong.

DOWN IN THE FLOOD

Ellen and I are up the mountain behind our rondavel, looking out over the camptown as the light starts to change, the days growing shorter now. Down below kids are riding bicycles, two boys per bike, coasting down the main road where it curls toward the Senqu Hotel, letting gravity take them. Bikes are a rare sight; not many people in town have the resources for small luxuries like these, and the Mokhotlong terrain is unsuited for casual cruising. As I watch the boys go, I can remember a time my brother and I rode like that through the forest preserve near our house—but we were adults then, not boys. In the quiet of the forest preserve, my brother and I were cut off from the world, blades of sunlight slashing down through the canopy and lacing our private glade with shadow. John pedaled and I stood on the back pegs, my feet perched on metal grips, my hands tight on his shoulders. If I leaned too far to one side or the other, we were both going down.

Along the way, we talked in the secret code of brothers, talked about big changes that were coming to our lives. We were two adults, not far from thirty—just growing up.

⁊.ᴥ.ᴚ

This has become our late afternoon routine now: Ellen and I hike up the mountain, stop to take in the glory of the camptown at sunset, then hustle back down to our rondavel before dark. We are well into autumn, and the high mountain air is frigid.

As the sun sets, we are moving quickly, pumping heat into our limbs. Ellen is telling me about a trip she took out to see 'M'e Masekhonyana, a grandmother in her late sixties, whom Ellen has been visiting for a while now. Three years ago, Masekhonyana's daughter and grandson had returned to her village, both very sick, the daughter in terminal condition. She died after a few days, leaving Masekhonyana to raise the grandson. The boy is thriving, Ellen tells me. *Nkhono* has adapted to this challenge, has helped him manage his infection and his meds.

I am coming to understand that this is a common pattern in the rural districts of Lesotho: young women trekking back to their natal villages to die. Many of the grandmothers that Ellen works with have told her this same story. As we clamber over a lip of rock, I realize it is Limpho the butchery girl's story, as well as the story of Kapoko's grown daughter.

It was a difficult span of days for Masekhonyana, Ellen says, back when her daughter and grandson arrived. The daughter cycled between bouts of vomiting and diarrhea, and *nkhono* found herself washing her daughter as she had done many years before, those long-dormant motions suddenly familiar. The muscle memory of soothing a sick child never entirely disappears.

"I was washing her again and again," *nkhono* told Ellen. "And the baby, even he was sick. They were both wearing nappies and I was changing them. I was changing the mother, then changing the baby, changing the mother, then changing the baby, all through the night."

For several days, *nkhono* worked like this. Other children in the village helped her with chores while she was occupied, doing laundry and washing dishes, gathering wood and cooking *papa*, fetching water throughout the day. When her daughter died, Masekhonyana turned to the business of raising her grandson.

In the villages, scenes like these play out in endless loop: elderly women raising small children, small children attending to the responsibilities of dead parents—just growing up.

ॳ.ॳ.ॳ

Ellen and I have come down off the mountain, breathing hard in the thin air. I head into town to buy some necessary ingredients while Ellen begins cooking dinner.

By the time I return from the Chinese trading post, the rain is coming down. I am soaked through, even with my waterproof on, and it will be at least ten more minutes before I make it home. A cow bellows at me from behind a half-collapsed fence, then returns to gazing mournfully through the veil of rain, mooning over a lost bovine love. I walk uphill as impromptu streams sluice down around my ankles. The dirt track is no longer a dirt track but a sucking bog.

Suddenly I hear some clamor over the roaring static of rain. There are four young boys running down the hill toward me, maybe eight years old. They run, screaming and hollering, then stop to shake their fists at the mud beneath them. Their cries are wild and hilarious. Each boy is sopping. I watch this bizarre behavior continue: they run, then stop to yell at the earth—sometimes exultant, sometimes slumping—then scramble on, getting closer to me each time. Finally I can see what is happening. The four boys are racing four flower petals down one of the impromptu streams, four colorful boats in the muddy torrent. The petals speed along, then snag in an eddy, sucked down for a moment, then pop back up again and bob bravely onward. Each time the petals get pulled into a vortex, the lead changes hands. One petal will be far out in front, the clear victor, then—*disaster!*—the other three petals slip past.

In the fading light, the boys are frenzied, each urging his petal forward. I watch them for a moment, then run over to join them.

"*O tla fihla!*" I yell as we run. "*Tiea! Tiea! Tiea!*"—these exhortations that Nthabeleng taught me as we watched the marathon.

The boys take this development in stride. It is possible that they recognize me as the *lekhooa* teacher out at the high school, prone to fits of unaccountable behavior. It is also possible that I am a stranger to them, but my decision to join in the race fits squarely within their worldview—shouldn't everyone be captivated by their teeming inner galaxies? Whatever the case, the race continues unabated, and we charge down the hill at the mercy of the storm, petals and boys alike.

FORTY-ONE MONTHS

Thato is a small sad boy who has come to stay at the safe home. His mother has died and his father is off working somewhere, possibly South Africa. His grandmother, who has struggled to care for him by herself, has brought him in. Thato is severely malnourished and HIV positive, three and a half years old, with a tiny skeleton's body and mournful eyes that swivel in their sockets as they silently scan the room, trying to interpret this newest confusion, this latest question with no answer.

Thato makes ten currently at the safe home. But what separates Thato from the other children is that, on some level, he knows what has happened to him. Most of the babies here—weeks old, months old—are too young to process their circumstances. They don't understand that their mother is dead, or their father by necessity works in another country. They don't realize that their uncle the drunk won't take them in, or their aunt doesn't have enough money for food, or their cousin is in jail, or their sister is nine and doesn't know how to treat abdominal tuberculosis. All they understand is that suddenly they are being fed five times a day and getting their meds exact to the minute. Perhaps for the first time, they feel healthy, or at least the absence of pain. But Thato knows.

ॐ.♡.ॐ

It is his second day at the safe home. I am in the bedroom, playing with the babies before they turn in for the night. I take my baseball hat and put it on each kid's head, let the brim slip over their eyes, lights out. Each one clamors to be the next to wear the hat.

Thato is sitting across the room, away from everyone, staring at me. I motion for him to come over and he looks away. After a minute, I scoot a few inches closer to him, then hold my hat out toward him. "*Nka*," I tell him conversationally, "take it." He recoils. I move back to the other kids and keep the game going. Every few minutes I try to draw him in. Every few minutes he looks away.

Soon it is time for the kids to get into bed, so I start to leave. Thato sees me getting up and breaks down. I am one more person heading for the door. He wails, holds his arms out to me, begging. He tries to crawl, but he is too weak to drag his bony frame across the floor.

I pick him up and he clings to me, a featherweight jumble of ulna, radius, femur, tibia. He digs his fingers into my clothing, buries his face in my armpit. His body is shaking. I can feel the notches of his spine. His tiny bones are kindling.

≳.ʊ.≲

Thato directs his mournful eyes around the safe home. Doctors have come and gone. He has started ARVs now, but seems sicker every day.

Sometimes I take him in my arms and we walk outside. He stares at the birds and the trees and the distant harvested fields like quilted yellow patchwork against the mountainside. A multitude of local beasts—cattle, sheep, goats, donkeys, horses, mongrel dogs—moves slowly past us down the road, an animate freight train.

Thato raises his matchstick arm, points at the mass of animals, and says something I cannot hear in a language I cannot understand.

≳.ʊ.≲

Thato stops eating.

Our medical support is limited in these distant mountains, so we begin feeding Thato through a nasogastric tube. This arouses a passionate hatred in his tiny heart, a rare spark of life. He tries to pull it out every chance he gets.

After a few days, he grows resigned to the tube. His eyes are veiled now, clouded over.

ॐ.ॐ.ॐ

For two days, Thato is in the hospital, a small cluster of understaffed buildings near the safe home—the only hospital in a district of about 100,000 people. Lesotho has no medical school at this time, no doctors of its own, so the staff here have come from other countries, mostly Zimbabwe and the Congo.

Thato's eyelids are swollen half shut, but his mournful eyes still roam and swivel in their sockets.

His grandmother is here in the hospital room, sitting silently beside him. Someone has gotten word to her out in some distant village, where all word makes its way, eventually.

ॐ.ॐ.ॐ

Ellen and I head over to the hospital in the evening. We are about to sit down to dinner when a deep foreboding takes hold of me, so we leave our food on the table. We arrive right before the end of visiting hours.

Earlier in the day, Nyamatukwa the doctor—an incredibly talented Zimbabwean, who often makes special accommodations to help out the safe home—had told us what to expect with Thato's treatment: what should be happening with his IV, his meds, his NG tube. Nyamatukwa repeats to us several times the orders he has given the nurses on duty.

We arrive and ask to see Thato. A nurse eating cheese curls points toward a room, then redirects her attention to the soap opera she is engrossed in.

We find Thato's bed. His grandmother is beside him, staring at the wall. None of Nyamatukwa's orders have been followed. The IV stands next to Thato's bed, disconnected; he is getting no nutrients, no hydration. The cheese curl–eating nurse has told the grandmother to administer Thato's antiretroviral meds, but the grandmother has no idea how or when to attend to this precision task.

The grandmother's silence in the face of this assignment—the highly specialized care of her grandson, while medical staff sit nearby watching TV—strikes me as a strange and terrifying passivity. My mind struggles to formulate a question that begins *How can...* but there is no proper ending, only murky cultural forces beyond my understanding, issues of class or education or etiquette or power or fear. Or maybe it is simpler than that: a grandmother confronting in silence that which has no real analog in language.

I leave the room and tell the nurse to follow me *right this second.* Ellen explains to her that—*If you don't turn this valve right here?*—the NG tube drains the medicine from Thato's stomach before his body can absorb it. The nurse seems to register this information as if the words are coming from the end of a long hallway. Then she turns the valve and goes back to her station. It is apparent to me now that Nyamatukwa feared this exact scenario, although it would have been impossible for him to tell us this.

Visiting hours for non-family have ended. We make it clear that we are not going anywhere until the nurses begin to do their jobs, until the IV is hooked up, until the meds come. We bring the full force of our whiteness to bear on the situation, and we feel—what exactly? It is hard to know. As Nyamatukwa taught me, there are some things that cannot be put so directly.

We sit beside Thato's grandmother—this sphinx, this cipher—as her gaze silently floats to Thato, then to us, then back to the wall. It is impossible to know what she thinks of our presence.

Thato's mournful eyes roll and roam. I take his hand and he weakly wraps his fingers around mine.

⁂

After dark, we watch heat lightning far off over the mountains, pulsing and rolling in strange silent sheets. The horizon is alive with electromagnetic ghosts, dancing ethereal shades of purple, orange, and yellow.

Then the moon rises and charts its flagrant path across the sky. It bathes the road in cool light and awakens secret life in the willow tree that hangs over the turn in the river. Everything around us is still.

We are sitting outside with some friends from town. The immense spiral arm of the Milky Way is bright overhead, a broad smear of starlight.

Look just there, someone says, *that blur beside the spiral arm? That is another galaxy.*

Something about the tangible sense of space—this galaxy beyond our galaxy, visible to the human eye—is intensely disorienting.

We're so tiny, someone else says, *so insignificant.*

But that sense of cosmic desolation rings false to me, feels like puny cliché in the face of such grandeur. Something about the abyss embraces, something about the absence is intensely present. A strange fullness in the engulfing emptiness.

꥓.ꢤ.ꢢ

Thato dies that next morning. He had been alive for forty-one months.

As best I know, Thato spent those entire forty-one months in some degree of pain. I can only hope that we gave him some small measure of comfort in his final weeks. I can only hope that we did not somehow increase his life's accumulated suffering.

As the afternoon lengthens, an impermeable fog seeps over the mountains, something I have never seen in my time here. The peaks surrounding Mokhotlong become hazy and insubstantial, a shadowy outline against the sky. By evening, the mountains have dissolved completely.

꥓.ꢤ.ꢢ

Where are the platitudes we fall back on when someone dies, those battered bromides we use to console ourselves?

We tell ourselves not to mourn the death, but celebrate the life. We exhort ourselves to bask in those memories accrued over decades, to reflect on the joy that increased over a lifetime.

But what joy has accrued over those forty-one months? What is to be celebrated here—besides the fleeting and guilty acknowledgement that Thato's life of continual suffering has come to an end?

᠈᠂ᢣ

Sometime later, we meet Thato's father. We are staying overnight at the rustic alpine lodge at Sani Pass, near the border, where the mountains of eastern Lesotho fall away precipitously into South African pastureland. The terrain here is cataclysmic, dropping three thousand feet across the border.

Ellen tells me she recognizes this man who is helping us carry our bags inside as Thato's father, a chance encounter that is not chance at all, but a fundamental part of Lesotho's recursive nature.

It is snowing, the wind tearing over the edge of the mountains and into the drop. Once we are inside, we talk briefly with Thato's father. When we tell him who we are, he begins smiling, the kind of smile that is an immediate response to pain.

"Oh," he tells us, "thank you."

"Yes, you are welcome," we say, a response so absurd and unnerving that I feel myself drifting up and into the wind and off over the edge and down.

᠈᠂ᢣ

One of the great and perverse joys of working for Nthabeleng at the safe home is seeing children come in ravaged with illness, eyes and veins sapped of vitality—and knowing that they will survive, that they will prosper, that they will grow fat and joyous and will one day throw a tantrum because a puzzle piece doesn't fit properly on the board. It has happened so many times this way; I have seen Nthabeleng will so many children back to life. That is how I consoled myself with Thato when

I held him—the brittle pencils of his bones, the mournfulness of his gaze. I thought about how surprised he would be one day to discover himself fat and comfortable and annoyed that someone took his ball.

What a great luxury—to have the certainty of knowing that the odds can always be beaten, that the house never wins.

Some weeks later, I see Nyamatukwa out at the public bars. We are both very drunk. His eyes are impossibly red, his smile as wide as the sky. We talk and talk and talk all night about soccer.

Mokete was once like Thato, maybe worse: his stomach a bloated beach ball, his limbs shrunken and skeletal, his only decorations those delicate curls of ringworm along his scalp, his spine like a string of pearls.

But Mokete is here by my side now, this curious three-year-old, cheeks fat like two golf balls, a smile around the corner of his mouth like he's about to whisper a dirty joke. He is wearing his red-and-white striped beret, something donated to the safe home. This beret has been Mokete's talisman over these last weeks, and he is desperate when he cannot find it. Today I find him lolling on his back in the nursery, one leg crossed over the other, hands behind his head, the beret pulled down over his eyes like a cartoon Parisian sleeping off his wine.

I steal him from the safe home, take him up to our rondavel after they tell me that Thato died this morning.

Mokete is watching me straighten up the rondavel. He sits on the bed with a half-raised eyebrow. He toddles around the room as I fold laundry. He examines a small jade figurine of a hippo. He is content to be out of the nursery for a change, but occasionally he looks over at me, trying to puzzle out why I've brought him up here to do nothing, this resurrected child.

We sit together quietly. We are beyond words.

א.ע.ר

I stand alone in the full dark, staring up at the mountain behind our rondavel, thinking about the baby that is growing inside Ellen, the silent galaxy of cells that will soon enough be a little blonde boy. Suddenly—from somewhere above, up the mountain where there is nothing—a snippet of an American pop song comes drifting down. I can't make out the words but they are achingly familiar. Then the wind catches them and everything is silent again.

IV.
WINTER
TAKING LEAVE

When school was done for the day, the teachers told me to come with them, didn't say why. It was men I had played Scrabble with that first lunchtime, along with a few others. We walked out together across the plateau, past the airstrip, not saying much. Maybe they thought talking would ruin it, or maybe they didn't know how to explain. Soon we came to the house where the headmaster lived and without explanation we began chopping wood.

Eventually I came to understand that the headmaster's sister had died: we were chopping wood for her funeral. She was a former teacher, beloved among the staff, but had left the school before my time. She was already sick, I guess. No one would say the name of the thing that killed her.

Before long we were sweating, my fancy teaching shirt plastered to my back despite the cold weather. These were large, unwieldy tree limbs, thick crooked branches, not the tidy stripped chunks of log you see in movies— this was my point of comparison, anyway, my prior experience with wood-chopping limited to what I had seen on TV. For a while I worked a two-handled saw with another man, then rotated out, then took up an ax for a while. We didn't have enough work gloves or tools for all the men gathered, so we cycled through shifts.

As we chopped, I thought about a passage in The Grapes of Wrath. During the Joad family's voyage to California, Grampa dies and the family is forced to bury him along the side of the road. As night falls, the men take turns digging the grave, chopping and resting, chopping and resting. Once

they have Grampa in the earth, the family asks the fallen preacher Jim Casy
to say a few words, which he does, reluctantly.

He says: "This here ol' man jus' lived a life an' jus' died out of it. I don'
know whether he was good or bad, but that don't matter much. He was
alive, an' that's what matters. An' now he's dead, an' that don't matter."

We worked for a while under a cold winter sun and then the
headmaster came out with some pitchers of water. He poured in flavor
packets and stirred up the punch and we passed it around the circle and
drank. I understood that these men had thought to include me in a ritual
both sacred and mundane, one of the many ways we navigate our days.

REQUIEM FOR A
DEAD DONKEY

The winter wind hits as I exit the Chinese trading post and grocery store, where all daily needs are met, especially if those needs involve canned fish spines, or a child's bicycle with pink daisy pattern, or an eighty-kilogram sack of maize meal, or a street-fight-ready butterfly knife. Innumerable dust-covered delights like these fill the aisles, which are patrolled by a friendly shotgun-toting Mosotho who no longer checks my bag for theft.

I nod to some familiar faces as I leave the cinderblock warehouse. The front stoop of the *ma*-China store is one of the busier places in town, a community crossroads of sorts. The large concrete porch sits under an overhang that provides shelter for the old grandmothers selling cheese curls, phone cards, *makoenya*, and other small-scale miscellany. There are ponies hitched to the rail, stamping anxiously as trucks arrive in dust clouds; there are knots of kids parceling pennies to buy an afterschool gum stick; there are local politicians making impromptu stump speeches. If you come during the right season, you can even see the enormous Caucasian Santa Clause that waves a slo-mo animatronic greeting to confused pedestrians, making babies cry with its dead-eyed nightmare gaze. Sometimes I spend hours sitting on the stoop of the grocery store, reading and people watching. I speak my garbled Engli-Sotho with shepherds and schoolteachers, police officers and trash burners, all the citizens of Mokhotlong who stop to chat and then continue along their way. It is a pleasant way to pass an afternoon.

I am coming up the hill from the grocery store with a flat of fresh eggs in my arms, the wind stealing under my down vest, when I come across a dead donkey along the side of the road. The creature is lying in front of a corral, set back from the road and populated with cattle, sheep, horses, and more donkeys. This corral is run by the Stock Theft Detection Unit—a division of the police, a SWAT team for cattle rustling, which is a serious problem up here in the mountains (cf. Moshoeshoe I, *Pater Patriae*). This corral serves as a holding pen for recovered stolen animals or animals broken off from the herd, shepherdless and of unknown provenance, donkey lost-and-found.

During the winter, weaker animals regularly die overnight, unable to survive the sub-freezing temperatures, and each morning the officers drag new carcasses out front, leaving them for scavengers. I stop for a moment to pay my respects in front of the donkey. This sorry creature still has faint hints of life clinging to it, or at least the appearance of life, which turns out to be nothing more than the wind running through its threadbare coat. The other animals shift in the late afternoon cold, standing behind a hand-piled rock wall and a fence of rough timbers. Skinny nags, bulls and cows in groups, a knock-kneed calf struggling to stand. Sheep are fenced off in a separate pen, apart from the general inmate population. The various beasts are clustered in twos and threes like an array of bonbons: creamy custards and milk chocolates and bitter noirs.

Strangely, the donkeys have all pressed themselves up against the interior stone wall, staring out toward the corpse like the bereaved at a funeral, their wide liquid eyes sadder than usual. Their unfocused gazes look past me, past the dead donkey, out toward the mountainous horizon.

What is most interesting, though, is the dead donkey's body. The devil dogs have not yet had a chance to tear into it, although I know that by morning the corpse will be greatly feasted upon. It is laid out neatly on its side, as if the creature had moments ago been standing upright when a sudden gust of wind knocked it sideways, mortally so. It looks peaceful, but staged—which is what all bodies look like in their funerary presentation. Here's the striking thing. The donkey looks somehow…deflated. Not skinnier, not thinner—it is as if the creature's internal air supply has whistled out into the atmosphere and left behind vacuum-packed meat.

I must now make a shameful confession. As I stand on the side of this mountain road staring at the dead, deflated donkey, I am reminded of the way in which I spent much of my time in high school and college, which was studying ancient Greek.

As I contemplate this airless beast, the Greek word for "wind" or "air" pops into my head: *pneuma*. This root shows up in any number of common English words, from *pneumatic* to *pneumonia* to *pneumonoultramicroscopicsilicovolcanoconiosis*. In an instant of linguaphilic delight, I realize that this deflated donkey truly has lost its *pneuma*, because in addition to meaning "air," the word *pneuma* also means "soul." And with a further nerdish trill, I remember that the word for "soul" in Latin is *anima*, which of course leads directly to the word *animal*, which again returns me to the side of the road, standing in a ditch in front of a corral for misplaced livestock.

In an attempt to save this from tumbling into some sort of pseudo-intellectual wankery, I will mention a final harmonious tidbit. In Sesotho—which shares absolutely no common linguistic or cultural origins with ancient Greek—the same exact concept applies. *Moea* is the Sesotho word for "wind" and "air," and it is also the Sesotho word for "soul."

I'm tempted to keep excavating for some half-baked ontological insight, but some things are best left untheorized. There is always the danger of thinking all the accidental beauty out of something. When stumbling upon one of life's strange concinnities, maybe it's best to appreciate it for a moment—dust it off, polish it—and then place it back where you found it, even if that is in a run-off ditch beside an animal carcass.

Beyond the corral, off behind the *ma*-China store, a ghostly moon is rising early over the mountains. Before I can manufacture any further poignancy for a scene that deserves none, the wind picks up— the *moea*, the *pneuma*—and drives me shivering home.

PAKELA THE GUARD

We are sitting outside our rondavel watching smoke rise from the fire pit. Reid coaxes the blaze to life, performing alchemical sleights of hand— it is something dull and dead and then it is not, crackling, scintillating, awake. Bridget sits with Ellen and me on discarded cinderblocks as we watch a gaudy sunset detonate across the mountains.

Ellen is telling us how she rode along with the outreach team today, out to the mortuary to retrieve the body of an eight-year-old girl. The child had passed through the safe home a few years back, before eventually returning to live with relatives. No one knew the exact cause of her death, some complications with meds maybe—the relatives had been accidentally doubling her dose—but maybe she just died, succumbed. Whatever the case, the relatives had no way to transport the girl's body back to the village for burial.

At the mortuary, Ellen says, the staff had difficulty locating the girl's body. They slid open drawer after drawer, the cool slide of steel carving the silent room. Some of the drawers had more than one body. When they found the girl, they wrapped her in a gray shepherd's blanket and laid her in the back of the 4WD, then set out for the village. The roads were rough and Ellen tried to make sure the blanket didn't come undone while they traveled, the truck tilting and rocking as they eased through the flat, shallow river.

In the village, the relatives had prepared a rondavel to receive her body. All the furniture was emptied and the floor had been swept clean.

Even out front the women were sweeping with hand brooms made of bundled straw, leaving patterns in the dust, graceful semicircles arcing across the yard. They carried the girl's body inside and placed her on the floor. In the next rondavel over, Ellen could hear the older sister keening and moaning, the sound of her grief drifting over the body and hanging like a mist in the room. Then they paid their respects to the family and left.

As Ellen talks, the sunset is gradually softening into amber and purple-orange. The mountains take on a hazy, blunted aspect. Now we are bathed in the kind of early evening light that reveals the hidden nature of all things, uncovering strange colors, plucking shades of lavender and green out of the red rocks.

Then the sounds come floating to us:

pop pop pop pop   pop pop pop pop pop   pop

"Hey," Ellen says, looking up. "Someone's lighting off firecrackers over there."

⊰●⊱

On Friday nights, we host a salon at the Senqu Hotel, a low compound of burnt umber buildings on the western edge of the camptown, nestled beneath an enormous red-and-white radio tower. We sit in the hotel's frigid and empty dining room—one of Mokhotlong's two restaurants—and we tell fantastic lies and teach Nthabeleng English curses and insults, which she deploys far more adroitly than any of us.

At its core, our salon consists of just five—Reid and Bridget, Ellen and me, and Nthabeleng—but we are regularly joined by any combination of the following: Nthabeleng's sister Kokonyana, who was with us at the marathon; an array of American doctors on rotation at the rural clinics; the Congolese and Zim physicians, who flirt ambitiously with Nthabeleng; and a cornucopia of drifting expats. Once we welcomed a vagabond Australian whose life goal was to visit every country on the planet—Lesotho put him at ninety-eight, cruising toward the century mark.

Tonight we are drinking whiskey at our usual roost in the corner, where we can observe the dining room in its entirety. There is not much to observe. It is just our core five tonight, and one lone patron eating on the other side of the room. Our long-suffering waitress 'M'e Pulani intermittently wanders into the dining room. She has made the terrible mistake of giving us her phone number, and so we text her relentlessly throughout the evening, since a meal at the vacant Senqu Hotel dining room takes three hours to prepare. We send Pulani pressing communiqués like *how r u?* and *luv u bb*. Our salon, you see, turns on the sparkling and numinous interplay of great minds. Pulani rolls her eyes at us as she passes.

As we sip our drinks and tell tall tales, the lone diner across the room occasionally looks up from his meal to watch us. After fifteen minutes of pondering our idiocy, he gets up, plate in hand, and asks if he can join us.

"Of course," we say. "Sit, sit."

An imperceptible *something* flickers across Nthabeleng's face; or maybe it doesn't.

My first impression of this man is that he is thick, his body wide and dense like an overstuffed chest of drawers. He possesses a certain gravity, and I mean this less in the sense of his being serious—although he is undoubtedly a serious man—and more in the sense that light does not easily escape his ambit.

His name is Ntate Pakela, he tells us, and he is a guard at the jail.

"A guard," I say. "That must be interesting."

Pakela sends a high whistle through his teeth, seals it off with a snort, and looks over his shoulder to an imagined audience. This is his only response to my comment.

Pakela resumes eating, hunched over his food, his arms encircling his plate. He is grimly thorough about his business and his eyes dart from person to person as his jaws work. We realize suddenly how long three hours can seem, then try to remember what we were laughing about a moment ago.

After a brief silence, and at some internal and unknown stimulus, Pakela launches into what is clearly a premeditated monologue. This monologue is, generally, a commentary on gender politics; more specifically, it is a screed about how women are very, very dumb. He holds forth for several minutes, gesticulating with his silverware. But the finer points of Pakela's discourse must remain lost to the historical record.

Eventually he stops to swallow. The pairing of Pakela's bizarre misogynistic oration with my portion of whiskey has left me feeling giddy and disoriented. I watch the outline of a thick bolus of food make its way down his throat, and it feels like I am watching this happen in slow motion, in extreme close-up, like some perverse nature documentary. I am trying to suppress inappropriate laughter. For a moment, I wonder if his speech is some avant-garde stab at comedy, but then reject the notion. There is unhidden earnestness—fervency— in Pakela's gaze.

I make a mild attempt at redirection. "Ntate Pakela, I am asking, how many people reside in Mokhotlong jail? Is it very busy?"

"I can't tell you that," he scoffs. "Classified."

Nthabeleng—who has so far remained silent, contentedly smiling—interjects: "There are almost four hundred prisoners at the jail."

Pakela's jaw muscles gather themselves into tiny pulsing knots.

"It is a matter of the public record," Nthabeleng continues, looking past him.

"Yes, thank you, *mookameli*," I say to her.

Pakela's eyes narrow. "It is impossible for a man to address a woman in that way," he says.

He is referring to the Sesotho word I have used, *mookameli*, which means something like *boss*. It is dawning on Pakela that Nthabeleng is our superior.

"You must forgive Ntate Moshoeshoe," Nthabeleng says to Pakela. Then she looks at me, the corners of her mouth rising just so. "He is not intelligent in the ways of Basotho people."

I lower my eyes penitently. "Yes, what the *mookameli* says is true."

Pulani arrives with our food at this moment, perhaps forestalling an outbreak of physical violence. Pakela takes this opportunity to tell Pulani that his chips are cold, that he should be brought another serving. While Pakela's attention is occupied with a litany of complaints, Bridget starts to tell us a story about one of the children at the safe home. But Pakela will not have this.

"Is it not wonderful—" he interrupts, addressing Reid and me. "Is there not something wonderful in being a *man?*" He delivers this last word with emphasis, hitting the table lightly with his palm. Something about this gesture makes clear what I should have realized immediately: Pakela is tremendously drunk.

"Is that not how things must be," he continues, "to have *bo-'m'e* care for our needs?" He locks eyes with Reid, then with me. "Is this not the job of the woman—to attend to the wishes of the man?"

Then, showing forth a smile of the greatest benevolence, he swivels to look at Ellen and Bridget. He seems unsure what to make of Nthabeleng, but he is clearly daring the white girls to speak out of turn. Ellen and Bridget look at each other, amused, then at Nthabeleng, then at Reid and me. I can tell they are both suppressing the urge to laugh in Pakela's face, to sneer, to snipe at this man who has overplayed his hand in such buffoonish fashion. But there is really no profit in it. They remain nobly silent.

Pakela looks around the table, apparently awaiting an answer to his question. Nthabeleng lets out a politic laugh, shrugs, and gives no further reply—a gesture that to Pakela means *What could these makhooa possibly know about the respect that a woman must show to a man?* and to us means *Look at this asshole.*

"Indeed it is a great gift," I answer after a moment. "It is truly a gift that we have these *bo-'m'e* to heed our commands."

Pakela sits up.

"Just today, I chastised my wife for doing the washing. Does she not understand that washing and cooking are tasks that only men can do properly? Things that require a man's delicate touch?"

Reid nods sagely. "And you must not forget the rearing of children, which is also the responsibility of men."

Pakela stares at us. He is silent.

He is silent for the rest of the meal, sulking. For a moment I feel a twinge of guilt. The power dynamic has shifted so abruptly—Pakela knows we are mocking him, understands that he is alone, that even his fellow Mosotho carries only scorn behind her polite silent smile. He has made his brute, bullish charge at our enclave and has been rebuffed through goofiness.

At some point, the check comes, but we have long resumed our stupid gags, our nonsense texts to Pulani, our abstract riffing. We ice him out, occasionally directing a pity comment his way, rarely waiting for a response.

In the parking lot, he is walking a few steps behind us, then asks if we can give him a ride home. "Of course," we say.

Nthabeleng takes us all in the pickup. Pakela joins her up front and we four *makhooa* ride in the open back, thrilled by the dark rushing air, the silent profile of the mountains, the glinting eyes of the devil dogs that prowl the hills. She drops him along some black road and the five of us watch as Pakela disappears into the frigid night.

After a moment, Nthabeleng pokes her head out the window.

"*Kannete*, that guy was a douche bag."

꙾.꙰.꙾

Of course, this is not the last we hear of Pakela. In Lesotho, this country that is the smallest of small towns, paths cross and re-cross in strange ways. Nthabeleng hears the story a few weeks later, because Nthabeleng hears all stories.

"That man, Pakela the guard?" she tells us. "He's dead. And he had just been married."

That twinge of guilt again, as if we are somehow complicit.

"In addition to his new wife," Nthabeleng says, "Pakela had a girlfriend. But after the wedding, this girlfriend said she could no longer be with him, that she would not violate the marriage. This made Pakela very angry."

Pakela left his house in a drunken fog and walked across town to the jail, she tells us. Whoever was on duty that evening gave Pakela his pistol, which he was required to keep on site. Then Pakela walked back across town to the girlfriend's house and opened fire.

This girlfriend, she and her family huddled inside. Surely they were very scared; there were young children present. Eventually the girlfriend decided that—in order to draw attention away from her family—she would face Pakela. It didn't seem that anyone was coming to help them.

She went outside to calm him, but Pakela shot her to death. He shot her five times. Then he went inside to beg the family's forgiveness. Then he killed himself in front of them.

It was strange, later, when we realized that we had heard all this transpire. We were sitting around the fire pit—taking in the gorgeous sunset, watching the color of the land transform while Ellen told us about returning the body of that small girl to her family—when the sounds came floating to us:

pop pop pop pop   pop pop pop pop pop   pop

A PARTIAL DICTIONARY OF
VEHICULAR MOTION

Bus: In Mokhotlong, a massive coach bus occasionally makes runs down through the mountains, heading for the capital. It departs at dawn and arrives in the Maseru dusk. As the bus embarks in icy darkness, breath steams out into the aisles as passengers vigorously fend off hypothermia. By the end of the day—having descended several climate strata—travelers strip off clothing and the well-past-capacity vehicle is now more Turkish bath than not.

On one trip out of town, I am huddled down into my seat, burrowed in layers of jacket. The TV monitors overhead are blasting *famo* music videos where teams of topless preteen girls cavort in fringed skirts with fantails of white plumage. Their tail feathers pop and beckon as they do the shimmy-hop and the peacock-strut over the bass line. In the back of the bus, women and men are drinking rowdily in the predawn, which is just one of the ways to stave off death by freezing.

Later we make a stop alongside a small mountain village. I watch as a man stuffs a trussed goat into the luggage hold of the bus. The goat is alive and squirming against its bondage, but the driver does not object to this living luggage. However, when the man tries to stow his unfettered dog in the luggage hold too, the driver says it cannot be. The man becomes upset, gesticulating angrily. He seems to be arguing that he has done this many times before. But the driver holds firm and eventually the man gives up, heading back toward his village with the small goat slung around his shoulders and the dog scampering beside him.

At a later alpine junction, a man is waiting with just a goat. He loads his caprine cargo without incident and the bus churns down the mountain, heading for Maseru.

Hitchhiking: Is awesome. It is practiced frequently in Lesotho and—since most vehicles are some type of pickup truck—it is relatively easy to do. Just hop in the back. Unlike in America, the recognized "please pick me up" signal is not a thumbs-up gesture but something more like a paddling motion, where both hands are extended, palms down, and waved in unison like flippers. Also different from hitchhiking in America: you will not get murdered by a serial killer.

Motorcycle: The Sesotho word for "motorcycle" is the brilliant onomatopoetic term *setututu*—literally, "the thing that goes tu tu tu." Ellen's *setututu*, a necessity for her work in some of the remote villages, is similar to one of the low-cc dirt bikes that she, in her Canadian childhood, was raised on, since she was raised by wolves. As Ellen zips off in the morning, helmeted and visored and padded in fleece-lined Carhartts, the men and boys look on in envy.

So when we arrive at the wedding of my teaching colleague Ntate Katleho, held in a mountain village across the gorge, it is unsurprising that a crowd of children has gathered, drawn by the call of the *setututu*. When we come to a stop, they cheer and begin to swarm around us. And then—as we remove our helmets and the amassed local children finally get a look at which one of us is driving and which one of us is clinging so femininely to the back of his kamikaze bombardier wife—the children start to laugh, slowly at first, then building gradually, the laughter coming in waves that knock them to the ground. They are roaring now, rolling on the ground in piles, pounding their fists against the dirt as they beg relief from this great joke, staggering and slumping over in hilarity—*It cannot be!*—devastated, ruined, the children in tangles on the ground like they've been hit with nerve gas—*No, no, no, it cannot be!*

Taxi: In Lesotho, the term "taxi" usually refers to a VW-style minibus, modded out with a third bench; it is intended for sixteen compact riders and often carries close to twenty.

In this particular instance, we have twenty-two. As best I can tell, twenty-two is the physical limit of a minibus designed for sixteen passengers and their luggage, which is piled in laps and in some cases reaches the ceiling. We are a dense cube of humanity. We are super-saturated. Then the taxi stops for a man who is waiting along the road. *Ah no,* I think, *no, it cannot be.* The driver—who is a very small man—hops out, and the man who has been waiting on the road takes his spot. *A driver switch,* I conclude optimistically. *Our driver must have reached the end of his shift. This man must be another experienced driver.*

But I am wrong. Our former driver, the very small man, climbs into the front passenger seat and perches jauntily atop the passenger-side dashboard, his back pressed up against the inside of the windshield. He is staring directly into the face of the man riding shotgun, balanced in a position in which the errant bump or sudden acceleration will result in intimate congress between these two. The new rider puts the minibus into gear and we continue down the road.

So then: twenty-three.

Taxi Name: Any taxi worth taking has a name, a creative moniker that conveys the vehicle's personality and brand, a name that represents the taxi's best self. The following are vehicles that I have personally seen or traveled in, an alphabetized list that can only hint at the diversity of fantastically named minibuses that prowl Lesotho's vertiginous mountain roads.

Accessorize	After the Storm
Air Force	All Good
Angelina: Born from a True Woman	Another Boy
Appletiser	Atlantic
Black 8-Ball	Chama Boy
Chedie Boyz	Chesa Mpama (trans: "Slap in the Face")

Chocolate Musse
Cure Ball
Deep & Quiet
Discount
Dot Com
Feel It!
Gadaffi
God Never Fails
Helicopter
Just Imagine
Master Peace
Me Against the World
Negotiator
Night-Bat
Oceanic
Perseverance
Play Boy
President
Razzmatazz
Red Sea
Salute
Sexy Eyes
Smooth Style
Storm
Taliban
Tears of Joy
The Animal
The Eagle Has Landed
The P.I.G.
Think Twice
Top Ten
Twice You Lose
Wonderful
Wrong Button

Cool Down
Customer Care
Diamond Lady
Dog Pound
Enjoy the Ride
G-String Dropper
Glamorous
Good Samaritan
Jealous Down
Loaded Weapon
Masterpiece
Mysterio
New Covenant
Night Owl
Peace of Love
Pig Cannibal
Poison
Princess
Red for Danger
Saddam
Sexy Boyz
Slow Poison
Speed Five
Take Five
Taliban II
Tennessee
The Boss is Back
The Heavens Are Telling
The Terminator
Thundersound
Toy Car
Undertaker: Dead Man is
    Back
Xonophobia

Taxi Rank: A centralized lot where minibuses gather to collect passengers for specific routes; an outdoor minibus depot. This is where Ellen and I are heading after we arrive at the Bloemfontein airport. We have been traveling in South Africa and need to make our way to the taxi rank in Bloem so we can travel to the border crossing into Maseru.

Outside the Bloemfontein airport, we run into a lanky driver with sandy hair falling limply across his forehead, a thin corn-colored mustache, and a face creased early from decades of smoking. He is happy to take us to the taxi rank. His name is Christian and he looks like he has been transported to this spot from the year 1982.

In the car, we talk sports. I am wearing a jersey from the Bloemfontein Celtic, a soccer team with a strong Basotho fan base since they play in the Free State, the only South African province that is majority Sotho speakers. Christian gushes about cricket. He is delighted by my ignorance of the sport, as it gives him an opportunity to philosophize about rules of play, strategy, and the general artistry of the pursuit. His English is crisp with a clipped Afrikaner tint. I ask Christian if he is originally from Bloemfontein. "I've never left it," he declares proudly.

Some context: Bloemfontein is the capital of the Free State, an Afrikaner stronghold in South Africa, and the Afrikaners are an ethnic group who—whether fairly or unfairly—are best known for their role in the National Party, the political party that ruled South Africa from 1948 to 1994 and instituted a system of apartheid based on white supremacist beliefs and fears of *"die swart gevaar"* ("the black threat"). The Afrikaners ended up in the Free State after their ancestors—the Boers—migrated there from the Cape Colony over the course of a decade beginning in 1835. Their ancestors were primarily Dutch Calvinist farmer-frontiersmen who left the Cape Colony after the British abolished slavery there, something that proved significantly detrimental to the Boer farming system. As the Boers journeyed north into what is now the Free State—a voyage called "the Great Trek"—they occasionally kidnapped indigenous children to use as slaves (or *"inboekselings,"* as they rather euphemistically called them: "apprentices"). The Boers saw themselves as divinely chosen to wander amidst the savages, heading toward some distant promised land, and they compared their sojourn to the biblical journey of the Israelites, who also claimed that God had sent them into the desert. The Boers eventually invaded territory that was part of Moshoeshoe's kingdom, which led to guerrilla warfare and general bloodshed throughout the region.

I am glossing generations of intricate political and ethnic history in a handful of sentences, which is always dangerous. Surely progressive Afrikaners today reject the abhorrent racial tenets of their National Party forebears and their Boer ancestors. But the racial legacy of the Free State must be acknowledged, since interactions between Afrikaners (12 percent of the province) and Sotho speakers (64 percent of the province) are still fraught with hidden and obvious tensions.

As Christian guides our taxi through the arid Free State terrain, I am thinking about Palesa, a Mosotho woman who got her economics degree from the University of the Free State in Bloemfontein. She told me about the time she sat down on a bench outside the admissions office, only to have the Afrikaner student next to her sigh disgustedly and move several seats away. She told me about the student group that tried to get the dorms re-segregated. She told me how the University of the Free State made international headlines when a video surfaced on the Internet showing white students urinating into the food of black cafeteria workers.

Of course, this is all secondhand from Palesa. Personally, I can only speak to the Afrikaner woman who let us exit her shop without a second glance while she rummaged angrily through the purses of the Sotho-speaking teenagers shopping beside us, or the bloated Bloemfontein hostel owner who joined us for dinner one night, only to launch into a lurid racial jeremiad after his second drink.

I am eyeing Christian in the rearview mirror as he deconstructs cricket gameplay; he is unaware that I have found him guilty of racial crimes against humanity. Eventually, though, I dismiss my internal kangaroo court. It seems only fair, considering my own country's horrific racial history. I do a quick calculation and realize that the

American Civil Rights Act predates the end of apartheid by just thirty years.

The Free State blurs beside us, rust-colored and flat. Christian—who is actually quite sweet—prattles on happily about wickets and bowlers and overs. After a moment, I remember that he is just a guy who wanted to give us a ride into town.

Soon we have arrived in Bloemfontein city center. But when Ellen and I explain that we are going to the taxi rank to find a minibus headed for Maseru, Christian suddenly becomes concerned.

"The taxi rank?" He begins murmuring to himself, starting to speak and then doubling back, trying to find just the right words for it. We are moving through city traffic now, sliding past the four enormous cooling towers painted with gaudy sunflower murals.

"I suppose—if you preferred, of course—I suppose I could take you all the way to Maseru myself, perhaps an hour, an hour and a half further—"

He is looking at us in the rearview mirror.

"I could take you to the border at least, although it would be rather expensive, hiring a personal car for that distance—"

Drumming his fingers anxiously on the wheel.

"It's only that the taxi rank, well, I shouldn't say *dangerous*—"

He laughs softly, looks apologetically up at us.

"But the minibuses, you know, and the taxi rank in general, well, it's simply a matter of—"

Christian sighs.

"There are just so many—"

We have pulled up to the taxi rank, loud and dense and jittery with life. He can't figure out how to say it.

We pay Christian and thank him for the ride, and he shakes our hands over the back seat partition. As we get out, he eyes us like a worried parent.

Soon we have disappeared into vibrant chaos. It is oddly comforting to hear people speaking Sesotho again. There are families piling into taxis, kids chasing each other between stalls, women cooking street food inside tiny shanties, and men spilling out of matchbox bars as they yell at soccer games. I greet a man in Sesotho and ask him which minibus we want—there are upward of forty jammed into this little square—and he starts laughing and takes my hand. He leads us to an unmarked doorway where we buy tickets, then guides us to the appropriate minibus.

As we walk, he points to my Bloemfontein Celtic jersey. *Maselesele* are not doing so well this year, he says, and maybe I should consider switching my allegiance to the Orlando Pirates. He pulls open his jacket to show me his Pirates jersey, emblazoned with that famous skull and crossbones. He is confident his team will be victorious this year.

Eventually we reach our minibus, and the man heads back toward one of the bars. Ellen and I sardine ourselves in among our eighteen new best friends. Out in the taxi rank, the man looks back at us and points to his jersey, chuckling and shaking his head.

GHOSTS IN SNOW & ROCK

There are men now, ten of them, in front of the barbershop—a metal shanty near the spot where the main road wishbones into two. I have never actually seen anyone being barbered here, but the shanty is nonetheless a hub of masculine activity. It leans in the wind on a stretch of road just past the cobbler's shop, Bad G's Botique, near the two competing coffin stands where carpenters are joining wooden planks into frames. Today they're building children's coffins.

The ten men in front of the barbershop are huddled over a game. It is called *morabaraba* and it is well beyond my comprehension.

"Eh?" I ask.

"MOH-*RAH*-BAH-*RAH*-BAH," one of the men enunciates.

It is a board game, a game of strategic positioning, involving two men, who move pieces around a spiderweb-shaped playing field, and eight men, who lean over them yelling directives and clawing their skulls in frustration. In this instance, the men are playing on a large flat piece of salvaged plastic, the spiderweb drawn on with marker. One man commands a team of pebbles, the other a battalion of old bottle caps. They are slamming the pieces around the board: *tock! tock! tock! tock! tock!*

I ask a bystander, who is vigorously coaching one of the combatants, how the game works.

"*Morabaraba*," he tells me, "only for *bo-ntate*."

He points to three bottle caps. "Those ones are *likhomo*, the cows—"

But cuts his explanation short to yell *"Butle! Butle! Butle! Butle! Butle!"* at his advisee, as the man starts to reach for an ill-advised piece.

The two men slide their pebbles and bottle caps rapidly around the web, occasionally stopping to flick the other player's pieces unceremoniously into the dirt, resulting in roars of approval from the onlookers. Eventually one man wins and one man loses, the winner having guided his cows to some desirable end, I suppose. A new contestant sits down, the pebbles and bottle caps are gathered, and the game begins again.

I continue my stroll through town. Behind me I can hear the men laughing and happily shit-talking, the aura of easy camaraderie hanging in the late afternoon air, this genial hum of conversation warding off the coming night, at least for a little while.

🪶🕯🪶

This is later. It may seem significantly unrelated to *morabaraba*, and maybe it is.

We are on our way back from Sani Pass, having hired Ntate J—a friendly man from the same village where Nthabeleng grew up—to give us a lift to Mokhotlong in his truck. An ice storm has encased the area overnight, and Ntate J is maneuvering through treacherous switchbacks, churning down sludgy tracks that run alongside the gorge.

Whenever we pass another 4WD, Ntate J stops briefly to chat with the driver. In his thirtyish years, Ntate J has worked as a shepherd, a tour guide, and an auto mechanic. He is the kind of person who can fix or procure whatever needs fixing or procuring, and he knows everything that transpires on the mountain: a reliable man to have at the wheel. Most notably—and this is wholly consistent with the labyrinthine internal logic of Lesotho, where all courses must bend and curve and intersect again—I realize, when he pulls up, that I know Ntate J from somewhere. He is the man our comically overstuffed minibus once stopped for along a mountain road, he who leapt into the driver's seat and took the wheel while the former driver went jauntily to the passenger-side dashboard and rode out the journey leaning into another man's face.

As we round a bend, we come across a group of four shepherds trudging through the snow, all wrapped in woolen Basotho blankets, all in gumboots, all with sturdy wooden *molamo* in hand, all masked in balaclavas—gray-faced phantoms moving through ankle-deep slush, eyes visible through slits in the fabric. These four shepherds are leaving a taxi, a 4WD minibus, parked in the snow behind them, and I wonder if their vehicle is stuck atop this remote pass. Ntate J calls out to them with the same thought in mind. The four shepherds stop at the window of our truck.

Ntate J is quickly involved in a jovial conversation. The four men pull off their balaclavas, their eyes bright with some shared joke, their faces shining from exertion, and now the five of them are laughing, the shepherds pointing up over a ridge. Ntate J is shaking his head as he chuckles. Now that their balaclavas are off, I can see that two of them have their hair cut in traditional shepherd style, close-cropped all around, but one man has a single blunted rhino horn of hair, another sporting two wicked devil horns. After a few minutes, the shepherds pull their balaclavas down again and set off, waving at Ntate J.

We drive on. After a moment, I ask if the shepherds' minibus is stuck in the snow.

"No," Ntate J says. "They are leaving it behind so it will not be seen."

This piques curiosity.

"But where are they going?"

"They are going to beat that man," Ntate J says. "They are going to beat him badly."

Silence in the truck. Then: "What?"

"The shepherd who stays on that side. They are going to beat him very very badly."

Ntate J accurately interprets our further silence as an invitation to continue.

"Those four men, they have found that the shepherd who stays on that side has stolen a sheep from the flock. He is the flock's caretaker, yes, but he is not the flock's owner, and so he does not have the right to eat the sheep's meat. These men, they have found the oils on the rocks, they know this shepherd is the guilty one."

Ntate J swerves to avoid a donkey in the road.

"They must beat him so badly. And maybe they will kill him." He pauses. "Really, they must."

Ntate J is relating all of this in an amiable and even-handed tone, as if giving directions to a stranger at an intersection.

"Because when someone is the thief, it means he does not want you to live. If the thief steals from you, it means he does not care if you can live. *Kannete*, he is threatening your livelihood. And if he does not want you to live, then you must kill this man."

His eyes go to the rearview mirror.

"Even you," he says, "if that man would kill you, I think you would kill that man."

We have no response.

"When I was the shepherd, and I was ten years old, the other shepherds once stole a sheep. I did not steal it, but I did eat the meat, so even I was responsible." He is lost in this surfacing memory for a moment. "Some other shepherds found us and beat us very badly for this crime. So badly that we went into the hospital."

The truck judders down the road, the door latch beside me rattling.

"You see, when you are the shepherd, you will eat only *papa*, only maize meal. You will eat *papa* once during the day, and it will be this way for six months. Perhaps one time in six months you will eat meat—*ichu!*—you will be so *hungry!* But once I was beaten, I knew to never steal the sheep again, even when I was very very hungry. And when I was older, I taught the small boys not to steal the sheep. Because the thief—*hei!*—it means the thief does not want you to live. So you must beat that man very badly. You must kill that man."

His eyes are on us again.

"And when you kill the thief, even God will be on your side."

᙭ᙂᙆ

Overnight, a heavy storm blows through Mokhotlong. The camptown is always cold in the winter but rarely gets heavy snowfall; this storm rattles the windowpanes all night and dumps half a foot on the ground.

In the morning, Ellen goes out in front of the nursery's big glass window, scraping and molding the snow into a waist-high mound. The children are pressed up against the window, the *bo-'m'e* curious as well, all of them trying to decode this latest *makhooa* oddity. Ellen is shivering in the cold. She adds raisins for buttons, small twigs for arms, finds a traditional Sesotho hat to place on top. It is the carrot nose that does it—for whatever reason, this is the tipping point into absurdity. The *bo-'m'e* are doubled over, the children jumping up and down, thrilled to get the joke.

Out there in the villages, out beyond the edges of the camptown, people are hunkered down in their rondavels, wrapped in layers of blankets, burrowed deeply into their beds—Ma and Pa Mohlomi are out there, Kapoko and Jesi too—everyone in quiet villages, trying to stay warm, waiting.

ᔕ.ᔍ.ᔓ

We are heading home soon.

Ellen is below, gathering her belongings. Tonight I have hiked up the mountain by myself. I am standing alone as Mokhotlong unfolds before me. There is the *pitso* ground where they held Tseli's kindergarten graduation, there is the Thia-La-La butchery, there is the Whitehouse, there are the *joala* shanties. I can see the high school buildings at the edge of the gorge, brooding like hens huddled in the wind, the property hemmed in by the sinuous course the river cuts through town. To the west there are men working in the Stock Theft Detection Unit corral, and past that is Nthabeleng's neighborhood, lit up where the sun has started to dip. The candy-cane radio tower marks the empty dining room of the Senqu Hotel. And although it is invisible, I can trace with my eyes the hidden footpath that winds through Mokhotlong's backyards. The metal roofs of the houses are ablaze with reflected light—it looks like someone has shattered an enormous mirror against the valley floor—and everything is far away and washed in the mournful distant light of the setting sun. It is the time of day when ghosts move through the terraced graveyards carved into the mountainside.

I am thinking about those shepherds as I climb. I wonder if they killed that man, if he died out there alone in the snow and rock. I wonder what it can mean to live like that—an existence of bare-bones pastoral simplicity, of violent biblical retribution, of psychological and physical extremes. These young men, these young boys, they float in gauzy oblivion across the mountain, smoking *dakha*, drifting for days or weeks without seeing a human face, out on some desolate peak talking only to their flock. What can it mean to be removed from human congress like that? Sometimes I'll find shoulder-high spires of stone up in the mountains, things that shepherds have constructed, balancing rock atop rock until a perfect tower rises from the earth: some way to pass the lonely hours, perhaps, or a system for counting the flock? Then I'll see an identical steeple on a peak across the gap, a hand-piled response: *I was here, too.*

As I come over a rise, I am suddenly confronted with a rudimentary *morabaraba* board etched into a flat-top boulder. The spiderweb design is clear, and some pebbles and bottle caps are gathered around the base of the boulder, the two teams of *likhomo*. It looks primordial carved into this boulder, ancient and chthonic, somehow predating the hands that engraved it. It is a meeting point for wandering shepherds, some place of communion. I wonder how long they wait here by this rock, hoping for a game, before drifting further into the wilderness.

I think back to those men in front of the barbershop, the joyous caffeinated energy of that moment, the brotherly badinage. Far below I can hear the activity of town—sound carries for miles up here—scrapping dogs, children hollering the wild fantasies of youth, the incessant braying of taxis, and perpetual song: schoolchildren as they walk home, *bo-'m'e* singing while they sweep out their shops, soldiers and police in countermelody as they jog in formation along the main road—the endless communal song of Mokhotlong. Up here on the mountain, the town feels imminent, haunting and intangible, a shadow world attempting to manifest.

AN ENCOUNTER AT
SANI BOTTOM

On the road from Mokhotlong to Durban:

Ellen and I are crammed into a rattletrap minibus, holding twenty, everyone bearing bags or people or both on their laps. The vehicle is stuffed with grandmothers and children, men traveling to find work in South Africa, and shepherds in heavy blankets—the whole minibus suffused with the rich scent of cookfire, as everything in rural Lesotho must be. As we jostle down the road, the subwoofers rattle the floor with *famo*.

Soon we arrive at Sani Top, the windswept border crossing between Lesotho and South Africa, about 9,500 feet above sea level. The border crossing here consists of a single one-story building where the guard sits forlornly, cocooned in winter coat, hat, and gloves. The height of winter has passed through—down below, spring is starting to emerge— but up here, the wind is unrelenting. The Mosotho border guard gives a cursory glance at our passports, a small nod, and then we are back in the minibus and heading down the mountain to Sani Bottom, the South African half of the border. I glance over my shoulder and see that sign one last time: *Kena ka khotso.*

In between these two border posts, we descend three thousand feet of mountain through some liminal territory. It is an hour's worth of driving, the minibus carefully winding over tiny strippets of mountain water. Then we reach Sani Bottom and pass into South Africa, which is almost immediately flat and green. It is clear who drew the boundary lines.

Our minibus scoots down the road, then past the usual drop-off point, the driver disregarding our transfer site without explanation. No one in the minibus appears to notice or care. We pass a rolling golf course on our left, part of a luxe South African resort where the wealthy come to play golf in the shadow of the Drakensberg Mountains. The driver turns off the main road here, opposite the resort, and heads down a dusty track. Just over a small rise, and almost out of sight of the resort, the driver skids to a stop amidst a stretch of fifteen or twenty rundown shacks stranded in the middle of nowhere. He jumps out of the minibus, again without explanation, and heads into one of the shacks. The minibus and its passengers remain parked in the sun.

In this tiny hidden outpost, a handful of people are milling about. We are just a few hours into the new day. I lean out the window—it is boiling in the taxi now, our twenty bodies pressed tightly together, sweat lubricating the boundaries of our skin. Chickens scurry nervously through the dust stirred up by our arrival.

A young man sitting in front of one of the shanties gets up and approaches my window. He is somewhere in his twenties, shirtless, with sweat glistening in the hollow of his concave sternum. He wears the blue cotton Jonsson workpants favored by manual laborers, his dusty and worn thin. This young man comes up to me at the window, our faces level; I can see a small constellation of scars arrayed across his face, his eyes clouded and dreamy with drunkenness.

I know it is surprising to see white faces inside this minibus. Ellen and I have lived in Lesotho for a year now and have never seen another white person riding in a public taxi. The white people who travel this route do so almost exclusively in privately hired 4WDs with khaki-vested guides doling out factoids through the speaker system.

The young man stares at me for a moment, swaying slightly.

"Where do you come from?" He speaks lightly accented, but otherwise perfect English.

I point to Ellen and then myself: *Canada, America*. Then I tell him we have been living in Lesotho—in Mokhotlong—for a year.

"Lesotho?" This seems even stranger than the fact that we are riding in a public taxi. "You like Lesotho?"

"I love it."

Something about this upsets him. His voice turns challenging, aggressive.

"What do you love about Lesotho?"

I think for a moment and say: the people, the mountains, the beauty of the land. I know this is a phony and packaged answer, but I don't really know what else to say. How could I tell him about Thato or Retselisitsoe? How would he understand someone like Nthabeleng or my vallies at the high school? How could I explain what it meant to walk with Mokati the bartender in that sightless black night? It is difficult, sometimes, to verbalize deep emotional meaning to an aggressive drunk in a small slum in an unmapped corner of South Africa.

His eyes are hard. He gestures to the shanties behind him. "You like this? You like to look at this?" His voice is spring-loaded.

I pause, then tell him again: I love the people, the mountains, the beauty of the land. I know this is not the answer to his question.

He stares at me and continues to sway, his eyes locked on my own. Then his face softens, almost imperceptibly. His gaze drifts off somewhere else. His voice is suddenly gentle, almost tender.

"I am too afraid of snakes."

I am not sure how to respond to this.

"In the mountains," he clarifies. "Too many snakes in the mountains." He waves toward the peaks behind us. "In Lesotho."

"Oh, yes," I tell him. "I don't like snakes either." I say this having never seen a snake in the mountains of Lesotho, but this seems unimportant at the moment.

His whole demeanor has now changed. Something about what I have said is funny. He leans against the minibus—the sides of which are still cold from the mountain air—and takes hold of my forearm in a brotherly gesture.

"Is this your town?" I ask him.

"Oh no," he says, "this is just where employees of the resort stay."

"Well, it's nice anyway."

"My house is there," he says, pointing to one of the shacks. "And that is where my sister stays." Beyond the shanties, I can see a small boy chasing one of the chickens with a stick. The young man points to him and says the boy is his nephew. He yells and beckons the boy over, but the boy runs off and hides, peeping occasionally around the corner of one of the shacks.

"He is too scared," the young man tells me and shrugs.

Across the road, I can see people out on the golf course now: whites golfing, blacks caddying. The young man lets out a sigh. "We were drinking too much last night," he says. "There was no sleep because we were drinking too too much." For a moment he looks exhausted, his face slack.

"Your English is very good. You must have studied it in school."

He becomes stern. "Oh no, it is very bad. I am not good at it."

"Then how can I understand you perfectly?"

"I am very bad. I can only speak isiZulu, which is the language of my people." He stops for a moment. "But I can also speak Xhosa and Afrikaans and English and some Sesotho."

I say a few words to him in Sesotho and he responds. My paltry Sesotho is embarrassing next to his, but he is happy to speak it with me.

"To communicate is the most important thing," he tells me.

And suddenly the minibus driver is back, running out of one of the shanties. He jumps in and revs the engine, still without commentary on his absence, and now we are ready to embark once again. The young man at the window takes hold of my hand. "Maybe I will see you again next year," he says with a quiet laugh.

He is still holding onto my arm as the minibus starts to pull away. "What is your name?" he shouts. He is loping alongside the minibus, holding tight. "And your wife's name?" I tell him our names and he repeats them, feeling out their foreign syllables on his tongue.

The minibus is moving too fast now—the driver has no patience for this game—and the young man lets go of my hand. "What's your name?" I call back through the window, but it is too late, the minibus rattling along, the music on again, and I can see him shout it but I can't hear him. He stands in our dusty wake with his arm outstretched in valediction.

EPILOGUE:
HOW SHE ALMOST DIED

I am on the phone with Nthabeleng, our voices tinny and muted, crisscrossing somewhere in the ether. This is back in the United States, where I awoke one morning to rather shockingly discover myself no longer in Lesotho. It was a strange sensation, as consciousness dawned and burned off the fog of dreams: a pang of loss deep in my viscera as the implications of the cream-smooth sheets became clear.

I am straining to hear Nthabeleng—trying to anticipate that lag when the words are nowhere, trying to avoid breathing noisily or even shifting my position, her voice so small in the back of the receiver. But I can see her exactly. They are rationing water in Mokhotlong right now and Nthabeleng is up the hill by the utilities office, waiting in line to fill some buckets. She knows everyone in line, queen of the mountain, and has spent these last few hours gossiping, laughing, working the audience, holding court. It is that glorious time of day when the evening sun sets the mountains humming, and I wonder for a moment if I'll be able to hear the horses charging down the main road, the cattle lumbering through the gloaming toward sleepy *kraals*.

Ellen comes into the room and I wave her over. "Hey, Nthabeleng, I'm going to put the phone up against Ellen's stomach. I want you to yell at the baby, okay? I don't think a child should enter this world without knowing the sound of your shouting."

"*Ache!*—*uena* Moshoeshoe—I'm not going to yell at a baby, you stu—" is all I catch before the sound is muffled against Ellen's belly. At the time, I didn't know if we would be back again. Our separation from Lesotho felt somehow permanent. I didn't know that we would return again and again, that we would always return, that we would live there with our own small children.

We talk for a while, telling stories about the safe home. Then Nthabeleng casually mentions how she almost died. She's been saving this story for last.

For the last few months, she has been taking classes toward her university degree at a satellite classroom in Thaba-Tseka, which requires a multi-hour drive through the mountains each weekend, and on this last trip, she almost took the Isuzu over the edge of a cliff.

"I was coming around the corner," she says, "when the stupid shepherd boy decides to take his sheep in the road. I had to brake fast but on the gravel this was no good."

She swerves away from the edge of the gorge and toward the steep embankment on the other side of the road, takes the truck wildly up the embankment. The truck settles for a moment, pauses to collect its wits, tilts on some unseen fulcrum—and then logrolls laterally down the embankment, heading for the road and the canyon beyond.

"*Hei!* Stupid Isuzu goes up the hill but cannot go all the way— this lazy truck! Then it decides to roll on its back and put its feet in the air."

I can see her face as she is yelling into her mobile phone—half anger, half amusement—surely playing for the crowd now, helping people pass the time as they wait to fill buckets with clean water.

"Then Isuzu decides this is a stupid thing to do—have its feet in the air—so it rolls over again and again."

The truck tumbles down the embankment and comes to rest back on the road, on all four wheels, inches from the edge of the gorge. Perhaps this is the time to note that King Moshoeshoe II—previous king of Lesotho and father of the current king—died when his vehicle drove off the side of a mountain. And perhaps this is just one more of

Lesotho's otherworldly distinctions: it is a place where heads of state can meet their fate at cliff's edge.

As she describes this, my stomach is bottoming out, that dizzying awareness of being powerless to protect those you love. Later, Nthabeleng would see that the car was wrecked, the roof smashed, hood mangled, lights blown out, passenger door inoperable. Later she would take stock of the moment, catalogue her injuries, comprehend her proximity to death.

I am sitting silently on the far side of an ocean. I don't even know what to say to her.

"Were you hurt? Did you get to a doctor?"

There is silence—that lag again—as our words ricochet off satellites.

"Hey *uena!* Do you think I was on vacation? I had to go take my exams!"

There she is again on the hillside, the citizens of Mokhotlong taking in her performance, watching her strut and yell in exasperation.

"The stupid doctor will tell me to go into the hospital while everyone else is taking exams! So I can go to bed and miss everything?"

And there she is again on that mountain road: the crumpled truck has come to rest at the edge of the cliff, the dust is settling around her like fine snow, the sheep and shepherd have scattered. Her seatbelt is tight across her chest. Her ribs hurt and her head is ringing.

Nthabeleng turns the key and the engine struggles to life.

She takes a deep breath, then heads down the road for Thaba-Tseka.

APPENDIX
LANGUAGE NOTES & MISCELLANY

GLOSSARY OF SESOTHO
WORDS & PHRASES

Ache!: an exclamation indicating frustration, frequently used in my presence; the word is pronounced with a soft "ch" sound

Bo-'m'e: women, mothers; plural form of *'m'e*; used as a term of polite address for women who have given birth

Bo-nkhono: grandmothers; plural form of *nkhono*

Bo-ntate: men, fathers; plural form of *ntate*; used as a term of polite address for men who have children

Bo-ntate moholo: grandfathers; plural form of *ntate moholo*

Boroso: sausage or encased meats

Butle!: a command meaning "Slow down!"

Camptown: the term used for the major town in each district (i.e., Mokhotlong camptown is the largest town in Mokhotlong District); in conversation, Basotho often use the term *campo*

Chelete: money

Chesa mpama: the name of a minibus I once saw; it translates literally as "hot palm," meaning something along the lines of "slap in the face"

Famo: a popular style of Sesotho music featuring accordion, bass, drums, and wailing

Fariki: pig; the word is from Afrikaans but is used frequently by Sesotho speakers; the Sesotho word for pig is *kolobe*

Ha kena lipompong: "I don't have any sweets!"

Hei!: an exclamation or verbal pause similar to "Hey!"

Hele!: a celebratory exclamation

Ichu!: an exclamation indicating discomfort or pain, often used for hunger or tiredness

Joala: a maize-based, home-brewed alcoholic drink

Kannete!: an exclamation or verbal pause equivalent to "I swear!" or "Seriously!"

Ke bo kae?: "How much does that cost?"

Ke kopa lifti!: "I want a lift!"

Kena ka khotso: welcome; literally "Enter with peace"

Khotso Pula Nala: the national motto of Lesotho, which means *Peace Rain Prosperity*

Kraal: a corral or enclosure for livestock; from Afrikaans

Lekhooa: a white person

Lekoenya: a fried dough ball, a fat cake

Lerato: love

Lesokoana: the *papa* stick

Likhomo: cows, cattle; also the name of the pieces in the board game *morabaraba*

Likobo: heavy wool blankets, often with elaborate patterns and pictograms; usually worn as the outer layer of clothing to a formal event

Lilietsa: to ululate

Lipompong: sweets, candy

Mafisa: a tribal loaning system for cattle

Makhooa: white people; plural form of *lekhooa*

Makoenya: fried dough balls or fat cakes; plural of *lekoenya*

Maloti: money; the plural form of *loti*, the currency of Lesotho; the Lesotho loti (LSL) is tied to the South African Rand (R) at a fixed rate of 1:1 and both are acceptable currency in Lesotho

'M'e: mother, woman; used as a term of polite address for women who have given birth

Molamo: a heavy wooden stick carried by shepherds; often decorated with elaborate and colorful wirework

Mookameli: boss (i.e., Nthabeleng)

Morabaraba: a board game enjoyed by *bo-ntate*

Moroho: leafy greens like kale or chard

Mosali: wife

Nama: meat

Ngaka ea Sesotho: a Sesotho doctor, a traditional healer

Ngoana: baby

Nka!: a command meaning "Take it!"

Nkhono: grandmother

Nku: sheep

Ntate: father, man; used as a term of polite address for a man who has children

Ntate moholo: grandfather

Papa: maize meal

Pitso: a communal gathering for important announcements, discussions, or celebrations

Rondavel: a circular hut, traditionally with thatched grass roof and stone walls

Seshoeshoe: a fancy or formal patterned dress

Uena: the second-person singular pronoun "you"; not necessarily polite, especially when Nthabeleng is yelling it at you

PRONUNCIATION TIPS

In Sesotho, the letter "q" represents a popping sound, while "qh" is a pop with a bit of aspirated breath. Both of these are impossible for *makhooa* to duplicate with any real proficiency, although attempts made in good faith will be met with amusement and general Basotho bonhomie. Most grammar books refer to this Sesotho "q" as a "click," but these grammar books are written by people who have apparently never been to Lesotho. The true sound is round and resonant and nothing at all like a click. Only once have I seen a grammar book with an accurate description of what the letter "q" sounds like, and so I will quote verbatim: "It is like the sound of a tiny stone dropped into water, or like the sound produced by the high heel of a woman's shoe."

The letter "l" can be tricky as well. The combinations "la-", "le-", and "lo-" are pronounced more or less as you would expect. But "li-" and "lu-" are pronounced like "di-" and "du-". The woman I knew from the Thia-La-La butchery, Limpho, would have pronounced her name ***DEEM-POH***.

Other common letter groupings include "hl-" and "kh-", both of which require more throat than you expect, and "tl-", which sounds like "cl-" to the uninitiated. And really, don't even bother with "ntlh-", which is a sound that violates several important principals of biological physics.

THINGS YOU SHOULD
NEVER SAY

As I believe I made clear, the word "Lesotho" is a euphemism for the female genitalia, and thus is a word to use with great caution. In general, it is best to avoid conversations in which one talks about how much one loves Lesotho, as well as any phrasing in which one combines "Lesotho" with descriptors like "dry," "wet," "large," "small," etc. These are verbal minefields. In discussing this euphemistic circumlocution with Ntate Baholo, he once commented: "My brother, we Basotho don't speak of these things openly, so we use other words instead."

If only poor Ntate Gappah had exercised a bit more discretion in this regard. Gappah—a great and joyous Zimbabwean who was working as a Civics teacher at the high school—entered the staff room one day and, addressing a room of twenty female teachers, declared grandly: "Lesotho lemonate!" Of course, you and I both know that he meant to say "Lesotho homonate!"—which means "The country of Lesotho is beautiful!"—instead of what he really said, which was more like, "Great vaginas, ladies!"

A POEM

For the discerning reader, I present a cento, which is a poem composed entirely of lines from previously existing poems. This artistic tradition dates to the third century CE but probably goes back even further, at least according to that gatekeeper of all knowledge, Wikipedia. Over the centuries, writers have stitched together these patchwork meta-poems from lines of Virgil, Shakespeare, Dickinson, Plath, and countless other poetical luminaries.

I have crafted my cento from a book called *Everyday Sesotho Grammar*, published by M. R. L. Sharpe in June of 1951. All of the lines in this poem are taken directly from Sharpe's handy phrasebook, which offers up expressions and idioms that the intrepid traveler will undoubtedly find useful in the Mountain Kingdom.

※.♡.※

On First Looking into Sharpe's Everyday Sesotho Grammar

Bastard rams are not allowed.

    He stabbed me in the armpit.
    We were disputing over a concubine.

You are charged with concealment of birth.
You are charged with contravention of the marijuana laws.

Rise, the court!

Have you paid your dog tax?
I have left them under my pillow.

Rise, the court!

My wife has run away   to a farm.

Are your periods abundant?
You no longer vomit?
Have you sores?
Does it burn when you pass water?
Do the ears not discharge?

He has pushed a mealie into his nostrils.
He has drunk poison.
He has been struck by lightning.
You must starve him to-day.

My side is paralysed.
I have cramps.
I belch foul breath.
I have hiccough.
I am flatulent.
I have colic.
I have vomited a snake.
I am breathless.
I am giddy.
I am depressed.
I cannot vomit.
I retch.

SOURCES

Bereng, Patrick Mohlalefi. *I Am a Mosotho*. Roma: National University of Lesotho, 1982.

Denoon, Donald, and Balam Nyeko. *Southern Africa since 1800*. London: Longman, 1972.

Eldredge, Elizabeth. *A South African Kingdom: The Pursuit of Security in Nineteenth-Century Lesotho*. Cambridge: Cambridge University Press, 1993.

Haliburten, Gordon Mackay. *Historical Dictionary of Lesotho*. Metuchen, NJ: Scarecrow Press, 2003.

Jacottet, Edouard, and H. E. Jankie. *A Practical Method to Learn Sesuto*. Morija: Morija Sesuto Book Depot (Original edition: 1936).

Lesotho Bureau of Statistics. *2016 Population and Housing Census*. 2017.

Mabitle, Pascalina, and Teboho Tsilane. *History of Southern Africa and the Impact of Major World Events*. Maseru: Longman Lesotho, 2006.

Moss, Joyce, and George Wilson. *Peoples of the World: Africans South of the Sahara*. Detroit, MI: Gale Group, 1991.

Omer-Cooper, John D. *History of Southern Africa, Second Edition*. Portsmouth, NH: Heinemann, 1994.

Puisano: ea Sesotho le senyesemane. Morija: Morija Sesuto Book Depot, 1988.

Sharpe, M. R. L. *Everyday Sesotho Grammar.* Morija: Morija Sesuto Book Depot, 1977.

Shillington, Kevin. *History of Southern Africa.* Maseru: Longman Lesotho, 2004.

Stevens, Richard P. *Lesotho, Botswana, and Swaziland: The Former High Commission Territories in Southern Africa.* London: Pall Mall, 1967.

Thompson, Leonard Monteath. *Survival in Two Worlds: Moshoeshoe of Lesotho, 1786–1870.* Oxford: Clarendon Press, 1976.

ACKNOWLEDGMENTS

My gratitude to the following people is impossible to convey, whether in forms written or oral, be it sign, symbol, or sound:

My dedicated colleagues at the high school, especially Ntate Mapola and 'M'e Mosoang—excellent bosses and mentors both.

Selope, Mamosa, and Tselane—for their wisdom and insight—and all the rest of the amazing TTL outreach team and staff.

The countless Basotho people who opened their homes to me, who shared time and stories and food and drink with me—kea leboha haholo-holo-holo ad infinitum.

Reid and Bridget, Brad, Harriet and Julie, and everyone else who endured extended periods of time with me in close quarters—condolences.

Jamie—pioneer, godfather.

All readers of early drafts (too plentiful to enumerate), who encountered this book at various stages of incompletion, incoherence, and stupidity—and who improved it on micro and macro levels.

Mary, Inara, Tony, and Rafe—your professional support has been invaluable; the joy I've derived from your writing equally so.

Leslie H., Crystal, and Rolf, whose specific involvement is hard to categorize, and who may never see this note; your support was fundamental.

Matthew Revert—artist nonpareil.

Rachel Vogel—tireless advocate, dispenser of good counsel and good whiskey.

Michelle and Leslie V., the beating heart of Dzanc Books, long may they reign.

Bo-Lephoto: Nthabeleng, Neo, Tseli, Kokonyana, Lieletso, Koenane— marvelous humans all, providers of endless hospitality, assistance, and wisdom, may my debt be repaid across many decades.

Bokang and Motsoane—never forgotten.

And of course:

Howard and Julia, Sheila and Jim, and my Gussie—whose love and support was overwhelming, and who frequently provided that most valuable resource: free childcare.

Mary, John, Anne; Dylan, Claire; Dan, Maura, Emily, Chris—fellow speakers of a secret language.

Bill and Mary, who gave me everything—your support, encouragement, and love are incalculable.

Sam, Eve, Mara—you crack my shit up daily.

Ellen—MVP.

ABOUT THE AUTHOR

Will McGrath has worked as a reporter, homeless shelter caseworker, public radio producer, UPS truck loader, Burger King mayo applicator, ghostwriter, and ghosteditor, in slightly different order. He spent twenty months living in the southern African kingdom of Lesotho, and has written for *The Atlantic, Pacific Standard, Foreign Affairs, Guernica,* and *Roads & Kingdoms,* among other magazines. His writing has won nonfiction awards including the 2014 Felice Buckvar Prize and has been translated into Chinese, Hungarian, and Japanese.